The Taiwan Success Story: Rapid Growth with Improved Distribution in the Republic of China, 1952-1979

About the Book and Authors

The Taiwan Success Story:
Rapid Growth with Improved Distribution
in the Republic of China, 1952–1979
Shirley W. Y. Kuo, Gustav Ranis, and John C. H. Fei

Economists and policymakers have long been perplexed over the way rapid growth appears to conflict with the other common goal of developing nations—more equitable income distribution. But economic expansion need not preclude equity, as demonstrated by the case of Taiwan, which experienced high rates of economic growth between the early 1950s and the late 1970s while simultaneously improving the distribution of income among its people.

This book describes how the Republic of China managed this balancing of goals and analyzes the reasons for Taiwan's exceptional performance. The authors illustrate how full utilization of the country's vast human resources through emphasis on labor-intensive production has worked to make Taiwan's products competitive in international markets and to make fiscal redistribution after the fact unnecessary. They also cite Taiwan's early attention to land reform, to productivity in agriculture, and to the spread of decentralized rural industry as important factors in the country's achievements. They point out that, although the specifics may change, strategies and policy implications drawn from the Taiwan experience should be applicable in other developing countries.

Shirley W. Y. Kuo is professor of economics at Taiwan National University and deputy governor of the Central Bank of China in Taipei. Gustav Ranis and John C. H. Fei are professors of economics associated with the Economic Growth Center at Yale University.

The Taiwan Success Story: Rapid Growth with Improved Distribution in the Republic of China, 1952–1979

Shirley W. Y. Kuo,
Gustav Ranis, and
John C. H. Fei

Westview Press / Boulder, Colorado

Copyright © 1981 by Westview Press, Inc.

Published in 1981 in the United States of America by
Westview Press, Inc.
5500 Central Avenue
Boulder, Colorado 80301
Frederick A. Praeger, Publisher

Library of Congress Cataloging in Publication Data
Kuo, Shirley W. Y., 1930–
  The Taiwan success story.
  Includes bibliographical references and index.
  1. Taiwan—Economic conditions—1945–   . 2. Taiwan—Economic policy.
I. Ranis, Gustav. II. Fei, John C. H. III. Title.
HC430.5.K885   338.951'249   81-12980
ISBN 0-86531-309-1 (pbk.)   AACR2

Printed and bound in the United States of America

Contents

Tables and Figures

Figures

Preface

Economic development of the Republic of China in the postwar period can be said to be highly satisfactory as rapid growth was accompanied by stable prices, achievement of full employment, and improved income distribution. In the early postwar years, concern with growth reigned supreme in the minds of third world policy makers and analysts. There was a feeling that equity could be taken care of "later," most likely via fiscal measures of government. By the 1970s, however, substantial disillusionment had set in. It appeared that the distribution of income was bad and seemed to worsen as growth proceeded. As the promised redistribution seemed to continue to recede, confidence in it began to wane; people and politicians began to express impatience and to talk in terms of choosing the alternative goal of equity instead of growth.

There exist very few examples anywhere of developing societies that have grown rapidly and at the same time managed to markedly improve their distribution of income. Taiwan is one of them. This book endeavors to demonstrate just how this was achieved—how the two important goals of growth and equity could become complementary and mutually reinforcing, rather than competitive, objectives. *The Taiwan Success Story* demonstrates that redistribution *with* growth is possible, as a consequence of the way growth is generated, and that one does not have to wait for an eventual redistribution *from* growth.

This book tries to document the specific reasons for Taiwan's exceptional performance. These reasons, and the accompanying policy implications, are formulated so as to permit an examination of their applicability or nonapplicability to other developing countries. Our analysis is based on a methodology developed in a book by the same authors entitled *Growth With Equity: The Taiwan Case*, published in late 1979 by the Oxford University Press, which kindly gave permission to proceed with this volume. Here we have tried to bring the data forward from 1972 to 1979, as well as to make the arguments accessible to the intelligent general reader.

We would like to thank M. C. Cheng and C. M. Tang for their help in preparing the manuscript and Karen Mikkelsen for her editorial assistance.

Shirley W. Y. Kuo
Gustav Ranis
John C. H. Fei

The Taiwan Success Story: Rapid Growth with Improved Distribution in the Republic of China, 1952–1979

1
Introduction

An Approach to Growth with Equity

The 1950s and 1960s have been characterized as exclusively growth-oriented; now, however, it is widely held that successful economic development should be identified not only with rapid growth but also with improved income distribution. Most economists and policy makers, however, share at least implicitly the assumption of the need for a tradeoff between growth and equity. The work of Kuznets, Paukert, and Adelman and Morris,[1] on the basis of cross-country cross-sections, concludes that, as income increases from low levels in a developing society, the distribution of income must first worsen before it can improve. Two facts support their conclusion. First, today's less developed countries (LDCs) generally have income distributions that are less equal than those of the rich countries. Second, accelerated LDC growth has most often been accompanied by a worsening of already unfavorable indexes of equality.

Historically, the record of almost all contemporary LDCs reinforces the general outlook of tradeoff pessimism. Taiwan, the Republic of China, is one exception. According to the best data available, Taiwan's family distribution of income in the 1950s was not very different from the unfavorable levels that plague most LDCs in the early years of their transition effort. But the distribution has improved substantially during two decades of rapid growth. This "deviant" record should therefore be of interest to academics and policy makers.

Although no two countries are ever alike and deviant per-

1

formance may be based on special circumstances, an examination of the relationship between growth and equity in a country exhibiting such an unusual performance can help to isolate the critical elements of that performance. Only then is it possible to judge whether the underlying conditions, which seem to have had the effect of virtually eliminating the usual conflict between these two principal societal objectives in Taiwan, the Republic of China, are sufficient elsewhere to permit somewhat greater optimism. Such optimism would not be based on the conclusion that achieving growth with equity is easy. Instead it would be based on the conclusion that some of the obstacles are made by man, not nature, and can thus be removed by changes in policy.

The Framework of Analysis

The problem of growth with equity can, we believe, be fruitfully analyzed in a historical context. During the third quarter of this century, the less developed world experienced unprecedented growth, a phenomenon accompanied by a resurgence of interest in the theory of economic development. We therefore felt that a natural way to proceed was to construct a framework of analysis that takes advantage of this new stock of knowledge. This framework consists of three dimensions: historical perspective, spatial distinction, and wage income versus property income.

By historical perspective we mean that the quarter century after World War II can be viewed in most LDCs as a period of transition between a long epoch of agrarianism and an epoch of modern growth. This setting of transition growth includes recognition of the dualistic structure of most less developed countries: Agricultural and nonagricultural production sectors coexist, and the center of gravity gradually shifts from the former to the latter. The basic phenomena include modernizing agriculture, generating an agricultural surplus, accumulating real capital to provide nonagricultural employment, and reallocating labor from agricultural to nonagricultural pursuits. And, for a small economy like Taiwan, export expansion is a decisive factor in the course of development, as it greatly broadens the market to create production opportunities.

Spatial distinction becomes apparent when we divide all families into farm and nonfarm families, as each of these two categories follows a different pattern. Nonfarm families live in and near the major population centers and over-whelmingly engage in nonagricultural production. Farm families are dispersed and derive their income from both agricultural and nonagricultural production, the relative portions of which depend upon the location pattern of in-dustries and services and upon job opportunities. Thus, the separation of farm and nonfarm households is a basic analytical device used in this volume.

Wage income and property income are the two essential sources of family income. The separation of wage and prop-erty incomes is indispensable for our analysis. Such a separation makes it possible to trace the inequality of fam-ily income to its various production factors and, in this way, to link income distribution to the theory of develop-ment.

The role of government policies is also crucial in the tran-sition to modern growth. First, governments must set the policy environment for private economic activity through their actions with respect to agricultural activities, trade, foreign exchange, domestic credit, tariffs, and so on. These actions — whether they work through the market by way of indirect controls or circumvent the market by way of direct controls — may be critical for the kind of growth path and the pattern of income distribution generated. Second, governments act through their tax and expenditure policies to affect income distribution after the fact of production. Third, because extensive education contributes to higher income as well as to higher productivity, the quality and equality of educational opportunity provided by the govern-ment affect growth and equity.

The organization of this book should be viewed in light of the preceding considerations. Chapter 2 acquaints the reader with the general story of transition growth and income distribution in Taiwan, the Republic of China. In the succeeding chapters we examine factors contributing to the achievement of growth with equity. We also attempt to forge a more precise link between the distribution of income and the theory of development in a labor-surplus economy. In Chapter 3 we discuss growth, distribution, and government policies in the period of import substitution—the 1950s and early 1960s. Chapter 4 reviews economic policies for export promotion and investment encouragement. In Chapter 5 we try to assess the relationship between growth and the family distribution of income for the 1964–79 period. Chapter 6 analyzes the effects of trade on labor income and economic growth. In Chapter 7 we consider the impact of taxation on income distribution. Finally, Chapter 8 presents our conclusions.

The study of income distribution is at a pretheoretical stage in which much of the effort must consist of examining empirical evidence. By sorting out the essential from the nonessential and the relevant from the irrelevant, it is to be hoped that the essential and the relevant can then be integrated with the mainstream of economic ideas, especially those related to development theory.

2
Rapid Growth with Improved Income Distribution: Historical Perspective

Economic development in the Republic of China over the last three decades can be considered highly satisfactory, as rapid growth has been accompanied by stable prices, successful labor absorption, and improved income distribution.

At the outset of the postwar period Taiwan was still a predominantly agricultural economy, with more than half of its labor force employed in agriculture. However, as a result of successful industrialization, this share declined dramatically over the following decades. The rapid economic growth was accompanied by improved income distribution: The incomes of poorer people rose much more rapidly than those of richer. Unemployment was virtually eliminated by the end of the 1960s. Inflation moderated in the 1950s and was very stable in the 1960s. Although it accelerated in 1974 because of the oil crisis, inflation was stemmed in 1975 and remained at around 3 percent until 1978, after which it started a climb in response to a second oil crisis in 1979.

Overall growth was accompanied by favorable changes in the structure of the economy. The share of production and employment in various sectors of the economy changed appreciably. The share of exports in gross national product (GNP) did not rise much during the 1950s, but it increased significantly thereafter. The major export items had been sugar and rice, comprising well over half the total exports up until 1959. However, because of rapid industrialization and export expansion in the 1960s, the share of sugar and rice dropped to 3 percent by 1970. Imports showed the same tendency. The import-export deficit dropped significantly and turned into an export surplus for many years during the 1970s.

The postwar development of Taiwan can be divided into two subphases, with 1961 as the demarcation year. The first phase was characterized by inwardly oriented import-substituting industrialization; the second phase was characterized by outwardly oriented export expansion. 1961 is used as a demarcation year for the following reasons:

1. Monetary reform was successfully achieved by 1961.
2. The multiple exchange rate was abandoned and a unitary exchange rate became effective in 1961.
3. The real wage rate, having remained nearly fixed, began to rise rapidly after 1961.
4. The rate of labor absorption into the nonagricultural sector, having kept pace with the increase in total population, started to exceed population growth rapidly after 1962.
5. The rate of investment in the manufacturing sector accelerated after 1961.
6. Private foreign investment started to flow in after 1961.
7. The average propensity to save increased from 4.9 percent in the 1950s to 8.0 percent in 1961 and 13.4 percent in 1963.

It can be inferred that a fundamental change in saving capability occurred between 1960 and 1963.

In discussing the historical aspects of development it is useful to select some basic processes that appear to be essential features of development. The basic processes thus chosen in this chapter to show a typical pattern of development in Taiwan, the Republic of China, over the past three decades are: (1) growth rate, (2) speed and pattern of industrialization, (3) labor allocation and labor absorption, (4) changes in productivity, (5) changes in wage rate, (6) structure of trade, (7) savings and investment, (8) income distribution, and (9) some other social and economic features. These topics will be discussed in the following sections.

Growth Rate

Growth rate measures the speed of increase in the production of goods and services. A higher growth rate means the amount of goods and services produced is increasing at a higher rate. In a developed country, where the production of goods and services is in excess of people's basic needs, a higher growth rate brings about an advancement in the standard of living. However, in a very underdeveloped country, where not even enough food can be produced to support basic needs, higher growth makes life possible. The degree of seriousness of achieving a higher growth rate is thus different for different stages of development.

At the close of World War II, per capita income in Taiwan was about US$70. Such a low per capita income has increased rapidly to reach US$2,280 by 1980. During this period, population grew at the high rate of 3.5 percent until the 1960s and at about 2 percent thereafter. Real gross national product, however, grew at the much higher annual rate of 9.2 percent on the average over the past three decades: 8.2 percent in the 1950s, 9.4 percent in the 1960s, and 9.9 percent in the 1970s. Due to the acceleration of growth in the later periods, real GNP doubled every seven years after 1963. As a result, real GNP in 1980 was eleven times the real GNP of 1952; that is, the amount of goods and services produced in the year 1980 in Taiwan was eleven times greater than that produced in 1952. This explains the particular phenomenon in Taiwan today that its people have not only an abundance of food and clothing for their own consumption, but also a surplus of products, which must be sold in the international market. For Taiwan, the Republic of China, rapid growth over the past three decades has meant significant improvement of people's lives.

Fig. 2.1   Growth Rates of Real GNP, 1953–1979

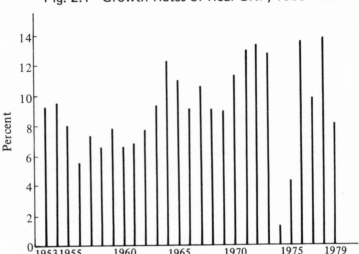

Speed and Pattern of Industrialization

The reason for analyzing industrialization in addition to overall growth is that economic growth over the long range is not realized by balanced growth of all sectors, but by relatively higher growth of the industrial sector against other sectors of the economy. Evidence for this can be seen in the rapid industrialization of the advanced countries during the eighteenth and nineteenth centuries. Japan had the highest rate of industrialization—higher than the United Kingdom, France, Germany, Italy, the U.S.S.R., Canada, the United States, and Sweden (see Figure 2.2).

The period of rapid industrialization in Taiwan, the Republic of China, was, needless to say, different from that of the above countries. When the period of industrialization in Taiwan is compared with the corresponding period for other countries,[1] we find that the speed of industrialization in the Republic of China registers the highest rate. Figure 2.2 shows the indexes of industrial products (in real terms) in a semilogarithmic scale, so that the slope of each line shows the growth rate of that particular country. A steeper

Fig. 2.2   Comparison of Speed of Industrialization of Republic of China (1952—1969) with Other Countries (1860—1913)

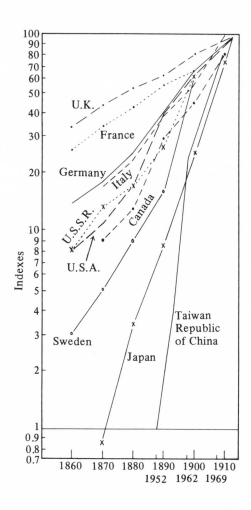

slope indicates a higher growth rate. It is impressive to see that the rate of industrialization in the Republic of China far exceeded that of other countries, including Japan.

Because of rapid industrialization, Taiwan's economic structure changed appreciably over the past three decades. During 1952-79, the share of agriculture in gross domestic product (GDP) dropped from 32 percent to 9 percent, while the share of the industrial sector rose from 22 percent to 52 percent. The rapid expansion of the industrial sector was caused primarily by the rapid growth of three manufacturing industries: food processing, textiles, and electrical machinery. These three industries contributed more than a third of the total manufacturing expansion during the period of light manufacturing expansion (up until 1970). They accounted for 35.5 percent of the manufacturing expansion in 1954–61, 37.6 percent in 1961–66, and 49.0 percent in 1966–71 (see Table 2.1).

We note, however, that food processing expanded first, followed by textiles and then electrical machinery. The growth of food processing was very rapid in the earlier period, accounting for a 25.4 percent share of the total manufacturing expansion in 1954–61; but in the two subsequent periods, its share of expansion declined significantly to account for only 14.6 percent and 8.9 percent of the

Table 2.1   Relative Share of Expansion of Food Processing, Textiles and Footwear, and Electrical Machinery Industries in Manufacturing Expansion, 1954–1979

(percent)

Industry	1954-61	1961-66	1966-71	1971-79
1. Food processing	25.4	14.6	8.9	3.8
2. Textiles and footwear	7.3	14.2	27.3	11.5
3. Electrical machinery	2.8	8.8	12.8	12.8
The three labor-absorbing industries (1+2+3)	35.5	37.6	49.0	28.1
4. All other subindustries	64.5	62.4	51.0	71.9
Total manufacturing	100.0	100.0	100.0	100.0

Source: Directorate-General of Budget, Accounting and Statistics, Executive Yuan, *National Income of the Republic of China*, various years.

manufacturing expansion. The reason is that food processing is an extension of agriculture, which has very low
elasticity of demand as income grows. Originally the major
product in food processing was sugar, which accounted for
45 percent of food processing production in output value
and 85 percent of food processing exports (see Table 2.2).
However, as industrialization proceeded and per capita income increased, not only did agricultural diversification oc-
cur, but the share of food processing in manufacturing declined. The percentage of sugar both in production and in
exports declined rapidly in the 1960s, although the absolute
amount remained almost unchanged. In the food processing
industry, canned mushrooms and asparagus were new products and new exports in the 1960s. The production of these
goods relies heavily on demand rather than supply, so there
is no way to have a continuous rapid expansion of these
products.

The textile industry took the place of food processing in
manufacturing expansion. The share of textiles in manufacturing expansion increased from 7.3 percent in 1954–61 to
27.3 percent in 1966–71. The strategies of import substitution in the 1950s and of export expansion in the 1960s were
decisive for the rapid expansion of textiles. In the later
1960s, the most rapid expansion was in the electrical
machinery industry, the annual growth rate of which was
38 percent (see Figure 2.3).

In short, the rapid expansion of labor-intensive light
manufacturing up until 1970 — particularly of the food processing, textile, and electrical machinery industries —
characterized a specific pattern of industrialization in
Taiwan. After 1971, this tendency changed. The share of
the three industries in manufacturing expansion started to
decline, mainly because of a rapid decrease in the share of
food processing and a gradual decrease in the share of textile
expansion. During 1971–79, the expansion of these three
industries accounted for a smaller share — 28.1 percent — of
manufacturing expansion. Instead, a relative increase was
observed for more capital- and skill-intensive industries,
such as petrochemicals, metals, and machinery. It is ob-

Table 2.2   Relative Share of Sugar and Canned Foods in Food
            Processing Production and Exports

(percent)

Industry	Export Value			
	1961	1966	1971	1976
Sugar	85.2	59.5	36.2	21.0
Canned foods	4.9	20.8	32.0	35.3
Tobacco and alcoholic beverages	0.6	4.6	3.0	2.7
Misc. food products	9.3	15.1	28.8	41.0
Food processing	100.0	100.0	100.0	100.0

Source: Overall Planning Department, Council for Economic Planning and Development, Executive Yuan, *Taiwan Input-Output Tables*, various years.

vious that with such development the center of gravity
shifted from agriculture to industry and, within industry, it
shifted from labor-intensive light manufacturing to more
capital- and skill-intensive manufacturing.

The development of labor-intensive light manufacturing
made many important contributions, particularly to the
reduction of unemployment and to improved income
distribution. These topics will be examined later.

Labor Allocation and Labor Absorption

Labor Allocation

The structural change in the economy was accompanied
by substantial growth and structural change in employment. Employment in agriculture decreased from 51.4 percent of total employment in 1952 to 21.5 percent in 1979,
while employment in the industrial sector increased from
20.4 percent to 41.8 percent during the same period (see
Table 2.3).

Production Value				Industry
1961	1966	1971	1976	
45.0	29.3	17.4	10.0	Sugar
4.7	10.3	11.1	8.4	Canned foods
18.3	22.5	22.7	18.0	Tobacco and alcoholic beverages
32.0	37.9	48.8	63.6	Misc. food products
100.0	100.0	100.0	100.0	Food processing

Labor Absorption and Elimination of Unemployment

The labor force in Taiwan was successfully absorbed, particularly during the 1960s. The unemployment rate decreased from 6.5 percent in 1952 to 1.2 percent in 1979. Unemployment rates from various sources, some of which have been adjusted or estimated, are presented in Figure 2.4. These rates give a general idea of the level of and changes in the rates of unemployment during the period from 1953 to 1979. The unemployment rate was high before 1965, but it dropped rapidly after 1965. By 1971, Taiwan's economy had successfully achieved full employment after a period of extensive labor absorption.

The rapid outmigration of agricultural labor after 1965 was possible only because of rapid labor absorption in the nonagricultural sector. In the 1950s, the economy failed to absorb all the newcomers. As a result, the number of unemployed increased during this period. However, in the 1960s, employment opportunities were successfully provided that absorbed not only all the newcomers but also some of the unemployed.

Fig. 2.3   Rapid Growth Rate of Food Processing, Textiles and Footwear, and Electrical Machinery Industries (1979 = 100)

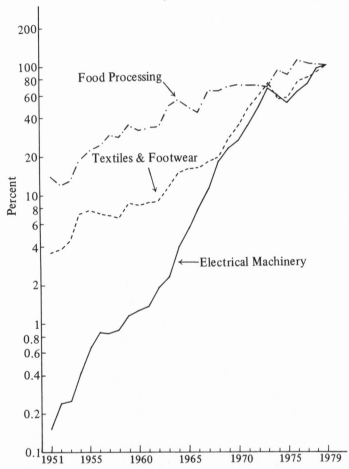

More than two-thirds of the economy's total labor increment was absorbed into manufacturing and its directly related industries during the past two decades. Three out of nineteen manufacturing industries (food processing, textiles, and electrical machinery) accounted for almost half of the total labor absorbed into manufacturing. The food processing industry, however, had a different pattern from the

Fig. 2.4 Unemployment Rate, 1953—1979

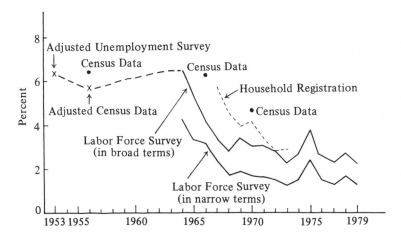

Note: The rapid increase in 1978 is mostly due to a change in sampling and statistical methods, which are subject to a further revision.

Source: Shirley W.Y. Kuo, "Labor Absorption in Taiwan, 1954-1971," *Economic Essays,* vol. 7 (Taipei: National Taiwan University, The Graduate Institute of Economics, November 1977).

Table 2.3 Structure of Employment, 1952—1979

(percent)

Industry	1952	1961	1971	1979
The whole economy	100.0	100.0	100.0	100.0
1. Agricultural sector	51.4	46.2	35.1	21.5
2. Industrial sector	20.4	22.4	30.3	41.8
Manufacturing	14.9	16.2	21.6	32.4
3. Services sector	28.2	31.4	34.6	36.7

Sources: Shirley W. Y. Kuo, "Labor Absorption in Taiwan, 1954-1971," *Economic Essays,* vol. 7 (Taipei: National Taiwan University, Graduate Institute of Economics, November 1977); Directorate-General of Budget, Accounting and Statistics, Executive Yuan, *Yearbook of Labour Statistics, Republic of China* (1980); Overall Planning Department, Council for Economic Planning and Development, Executive Yuan.

other two labor-absorbing industries. It registered the largest share of labor absorption in the 1960s but ceased to be a labor-absorbing industry after 1965. The electrical machinery industry then took the place of the food processing industry in labor absorption.

The "critical minimum effort" analysis of Professors Fei and Ranis contends that

> productivity in the agricultural sector must rise sufficiently so that a smaller fraction of the total population can support the entire economy with food and raw materials, thus enabling agricultural workers to be released; simultaneously, the industrial sector must expand sufficiently to provide employment opportunities for released workers. If the combined forces of capital accumulation and innovation yield a rate of labor allocation in excess of the rate of population growth, the economy may be considered to be successful in the development effort in the sense that the center of gravity is continuously shifted towards the industrial sector.[2]

The condition of critical minimum effort is therefore given as a growth rate of nonagricultural labor higher than that of the population.

The absorption of labor by the nonagricultural sector can be observed in Figure 2.5. The rate of labor absorption in the nonagricultural sector did not exceed the population growth rate before 1957. That is, no single year had reached the standard required by the critical minimum effort. But after 1957, not only was the condition satisfied every year, but the growth rate of nonagricultural employment far exceeded that of the population.

The growth of employment registered a higher rate after 1961, particularly for secondary industry. The increase in capital stock showed the same tendency. The higher speed of capital accumulation in the manufacturing sector caused a rapid increase in capital intensity in manufacturing after 1961. The growth rate of capital stock in manufacturing in the 1960s rose as high as 14.8 percent, while that of labor was 6.3 percent. As a result, the per worker use of capital grew at the high rate of 7.9 percent. Real wages in manu-

Fig. 2.5 Labor Absorption in the Nonagricultural Sector

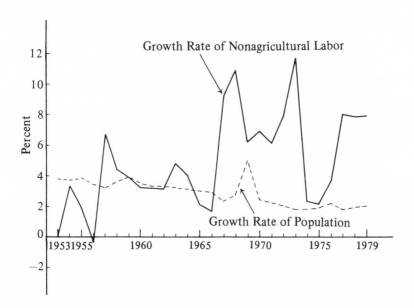

facturing went up gradually during 1961–71 and rose rapidly after 1971. This is due mainly to the fact that Taiwan's economy reached the "turning point" in 1968 and achieved full employment by 1971.

Changes in Productivity

An increase in labor productivity is essential for the improvement of life; only the increase of labor productivity can raise real wages. The achievement of both stability and rapid growth at the same time in the past three decades in Taiwan was possible only because of a significant rise in labor productivity. The industrial sector had a substantial increase in productivity from 1953 to 1968 (see Table 2.4). Labor productivity in the industrial sector in 1979 grew to 5.2 times that of 1952. During the same period the labor productivity of the agriculture and services industries increased to 2.9 and 3.1 times, respectively, over their 1952 levels. This substantial increase can be attributed to such

18

Table 2.4   Annual Growth Rate of Labor Productivity

(percent)

Period	Whole Economy	Agriculture	Industry	Services
1953-68	5.3	3.6	7.5	4.1
1968-78	5.6	4.2	4.3	4.5

Note: The data are three-year moving averages.
Sources: Directorate-General of Budget, Accounting and Statistics, Executive Yuan, *National Income of the Republic of China* (1980); Shirley W. Y. Kuo, "Labor absorption in Taiwan, 1954-1971," *Economic Essays,* vol. 7 (Taipei: National Taiwan University, Graduate Institute of Economics, November 1977); Directorate-General of Budget, Accounting and Statistics, Executive Yuan, *Yearbook of Labour Statistics, Republic of China* (1980).

Fig. 2.6   Indexes of Productivity (1952 = 100)

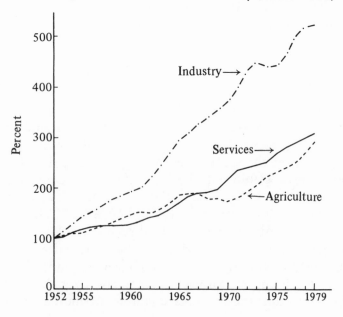

factors as the use of high-efficiency machinery, the introduction of new equipment, improvements in management, and an advancement of workers' knowledge. One point that deserves attention is that, despite the decrease in agricultural output in 1968, labor productivity still increased. This indicates that one reason for the reduction in agricultural output in 1968 was withdrawal of the labor force from the agricultural sector.

In short, technological improvement was the most essential factor in past development in Taiwan, the Republic of China. Various studies show that technological improvements account for about 50 percent of nonagricultural growth[3] and 36 percent of agricultural growth.[4]

Changes in Wage Rates

If the ultimate purpose of economic development is the improvement of the general standard of living, then an increase in wages should be regarded as a direct and efficient means of achieving this purpose. In recent years real wage increases have been generally suppressed all over the world. This is because the rate of increase in wages has far exceeded the rate of increase in labor productivity, causing inflation. The ideal situation would be one in which real wages increased at the same rate as productivity.

In the 1950s, Taiwan's economy was still in a state of surplus labor. In this situation, although the real wage may rise, the level of wages will, nonetheless, be kept at subsistence level. The significance of achieving full employment is not only that jobs will be available for everyone, but also that the real wage can rise with increasing productivity, so the fruits of economic development can be more evenly distributed to all participants.

Economists call the point when the real wage starts to rise in accord with increases in labor productivity the turning point. The turning point of the Taiwan economy is identified as the year 1968. Since then, real wages have been generally increasing at a higher rate than labor productivity. In addition to this, the wage rate of manufacturing after

Table 2.5   Annual Growth Rate of Real Wages

(percent)

Period	Agriculture	Manufacturing
1953-68	3.4	4.2
1968-78	7.9	10.8

Note: The data are three-year moving averages.
Sources: Council for Agricultural Planning and Development, Executive Yuan; Manpower Planning Committee, Council for Economic Planning and Development, Executive Yuan, *Statistics of Wages of Agriculture, Taiwan District, the Republic of China, 1961-1979* (May 1980); Overall Planning Department, Economic Planning Council, Executive Yuan, *Adjusted Statistics of Wages of Manufacturing, Taiwan District, the Republic of China, I. 1952–IV. 1976* (July 1977); Directorate-General of Budget, Accounting and Statistics, Executive Yuan, *Yearbook of Labour Statistics, Republic of China*, (1980).

1968 went up much faster than that of other sectors, reflecting rapid industrialization (see Figure 2.7). This phenomenon provided a good stimulus for absorption of the labor force both from the pool of newcomers and from the agricultural sector. During the critical period of 1966–71, the labor force was quite rapidly absorbed by the lower-wage industries in which unskilled labor constitutes a relatively large proportion of those employed.[5] That is, the labor force was more rapidly absorbed into more labor-intensive and lower-productivity industries, making possible greater use of unskilled labor.

One point we may note is that the increased use of unskilled labor during the 1966–71 period seems to have caused the wage rate for unskilled labor to rise more rapidly than that for skilled labor. Although wage statistics in Taiwan are far from sufficient and accurate for the purpose of comparing the wages of skilled and unskilled labor, some observations can be made based on the indexes of salaries and wages classified by staff and worker and by male and female laborers. The statistics show that the wage rate of workers rose more rapidly than that of staff in the manufacturing and textile industries and that the wage rate of female workers increased more than that of males in some

Fig. 2.7 Indexes of Real Wage (1952 = 100)

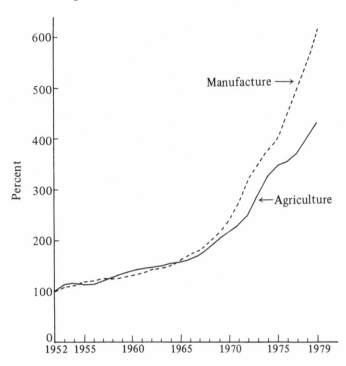

industries (see Tables 2.6 and 2.7). These phenomena deserve further attention.

We also note that the increase of manufacturing real wages in the 1950s was trivial, only around 2 percent per year. However, it rose to around 5–6 percent in the 1960s. Furthermore, the increase in manufacturing real wages accelerated to become nearly 10 percent in the 1970s. Again, the wage rates for workers went up faster than those for staff throughout the whole period.

Structure of Trade

Exports and imports have played an important role in the development of Taiwan's economy. The shares of exports and imports in GNP were 50 percent and 46 percent, respec-

Table 2.6   Average Salaries and Wages (1968 = 100)

Year	Manufacturing		Textiles	
	Staff	Worker	Staff	Worker
1968	100.0	100.0	100.0	100.0
1969	112.2	110.8	119.6	122.2
1970	122.5	125.3	129.8	143.5
1971	136.3	137.0	134.2	159.0
1972	144.4	148.9	138.2	177.0

Source: Department of Statistics, Ministry of Economic Affairs, *Taiwan Industrial Production Statistics Monthly, Republic of China* (April 1973).

Table 2.7   Average Wages by Industry and by Sex, 1972
(1964 = 100)

Industry	Male	Female
Manufacturing	203.2	203.0
Textiles	210.0	215.8
Electricity, gas, water and sanitary services	157.8	180.4
Transportation and communication	225.2	262.9

Source: Department of Reconstruction, Taiwan Provincial Government, Republic of China, *Report of Taiwan Labour Statistics* (1973).

Table 2.8   Growth Rates of Manufacturing Real Wages
and Output

(percent)

Period	Growth Rate of Manufacturing Real Wage		Growth Rate of Manufacturing Output (Value Added)
	Staff	Worker	
1952-60	2.0	2.7	12.5
1961-70	5.3	6.2	15.5
1971-78	9.3	10.7	11.5

Note: Output data are three-year moving averages.
Sources: Overall Planning Department, Economic Planning Council, Executive Yuan, *Adjusted Statistics of Wages of Manufacturing, Taiwan District, the Republic of China, I.1952 – IV.1976* (July 1977); Directorate-General of Budget, Accounting and Statistics, Executive Yuan, *Yearbook of Labour Statistics, Republic of China* (1980); Directorate-General of Budget, Accounting and Statistics, Executive Yuan, *National Income of the Republic of China* (1980).

tively, in 1979. With the transformation of the economic structure, the composition of exports has shown a marked change. Exports of agricultural products decreased from 92 percent of total exports in 1952 to 9 percent in 1979, while exports of industrial products increased from 8 percent to 91 percent. In 1952, rice and sugar accounted for 74 percent of total exports; however, rapid industrialization in the 1960s brought this share down to 3 percent in 1970.

The rapid growth of Taiwan's exports was led by manufactures. Manufactured exports accounted for about 42 percent of total manufacturing production in 1976. Food processing was the most important manufacturing industry in the early period. In 1956, food processing accounted for 54 percent of manufacturing production and 80 percent of manufacturing exports; however, the shares had decreased to 12 percent and 8 percent, respectively, by 1976. The textile industry expanded its share of production from 6 percent to 27 percent and its share of exports from 6 percent to 29 percent over the same period. The most rapid expansion

Fig. 2.8   Export Structure

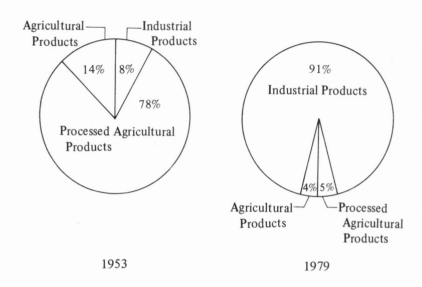

1953   1979

in both production and exports was observed in electronics. Thus, in 1979 the exports of textiles and electronics amounted to US$6.5 billion, about 41 percent of total exports. Exports of intermediate goods have tended to decline, and final goods have generally increased.

The rapid growth in manufacturing was reflected in and was accelerated by the expansion of foreign trade. On the other hand, the improvement and the output increase in the domestic manufacturing industries caused exports – in particular, textiles, electronics, and electrical machinery – to expand.

With exports of US$16.1 billion and imports of US$14.8 billion in 1979, the Republic of China was the twenty-first largest trading country in the world and the ninth largest trading partner of the United States. The United States and Japan together account for more than half of world trade volume.

In 1979, exports to the United States amounted to US$5.7 billion and imports, US$3.4 billion. Exports to Japan were

US$2.2 billion and imports, US$4.6 billion. Using 1971 as the demarcation year to divide the period 1961–79 in two, we find that the growth rate of total exports in the second period was faster than that in the first (see Table 2.9). Also, we find that exports to the United States grew at a much faster rate than those to other destinations in the first period, which brought about a government policy to diversify destinations. Its success is shown by the reduction of the growth rate of exports to the United States from 35.0 percent in the first period to 26.6 percent in the second, while the growth rate of exports to Japan increased from 15.8 percent to 31.9 percent and that to Europe increased from 26.0 percent to 34.5 percent. This diversification of export destinations changed the export structure, as is shown in Table 2.10.

Growth rates of imports, on the other hand, underwent a different pattern. Imports from the United States increased at rates of 12.0 percent in the first period and 30.2 percent in the second. The growth rate of imports from Japan has remained at about 24 percent, and that from Europe increased from 19.6 percent to 31.4 percent (see Table 2.11).

The trade dependency of the Taiwan economy grew significantly over the past three decades. The percentage of exports in GNP increased from 9 percent in 1952 to 49 percent in 1980; that of imports, from 15 percent to 49 percent.

The 1950s was an era of trade deficit. The trade deficit was often about 6 percent of GNP and sometimes even reached 10 percent. During this period, U.S. aid was relied on greatly to finance imports. Up until 1957, the imports financed by U.S. aid exceeded 40 percent of total imports every year. U.S. aid was terminated in 1965. By one year before termination, the imports financed by U.S. aid had decreased to 10 percent of total imports, and after the termination of U.S. aid, the economy moved into the "take off" stage and basically shifted to a trade surplus rather than a trade deficit. Despite the oil crisis, large trade surpluses occurred during 1976–79. The trade surplus of 1978, in fact, was 6.2 percent of GNP. In order to avoid negative effects on money supply and price stability, the government took

Table 2.9   Growth Rate of Exports by Destination

(percent)

Period	Total	U.S.	Japan	Europe	Others
1961-71	26.6	35.0	15.8	26.0	25.8
1971-79	29.3	26.6	31.9	34.5	30.2
1961-79	27.8	31.2	22.7	29.7	27.8

Source: Department of Statistics, Ministry of Finance, *Monthly Statistics of Exports and Imports, the Republic of China* (January 1981).

Table 2.10   Structure of Exports by Destination

(percent)

Year	U.S.	Japan	Europe	Others
1961	21.9	29.0	6.3	42.8
1971	41.7	11.9	6.1	40.3
1979	35.1	14.0	8.3	42.6

Source: Same as Table 2.9.

Table 2.11   Growth Rate of Imports by Import Origin

(percent)

Period	Total	U.S.	Japan	Europe	Others
1961-71	19.1	12.0	23.6	19.6	21.2
1971-79	29.7	30.2	23.8	31.4	36.1
1961-79	23.7	19.8	23.7	24.7	27.6

Source: Same as Table 2.9.

Fig. 2.9 Import Structure

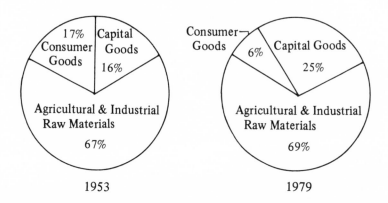

1953

1979

various import liberalization measures. By 1980, the trade surplus had been reduced to US$77 million.

Savings and Investment

"Take Off" and Sustained Growth

According to Professor W. W. Rostow, after a country's net investment comprises more than 10 percent of the national income, the country can be regarded as having satisfied the necessary condition for "take off." Although a high ratio of domestic investment to national income can stimulate economic growth through the acceleration of capital accumulation, the most important consideration for take off is sufficient domestic savings. In this respect, Taiwan's economy did not satisfy such conditions before 1962, as the average ratio of net domestic savings to national income from 1951 through 1959 was only 5 percent and from 1960 to 1962, 8 percent. However, the savings ratio jumped to 13 percent and more after 1963. Thus, we may say that the economy began to meet the necessary conditions for take off in 1963.

The savings ratio in Taiwan in recent years has been very

Table 2.12 Ratios of Domestic Savings and Investment

(percent)

Year	Ratio of Net Domestic Savings to NNP	Ratio of Net Investment to NNP	Ratio of Net Domestic Savings to Net Investment
1951	5.3	10.9	48.6
1952	5.2	12.5	41.6
1953	5.0	11.1	45.0
1954	3.3	13.5	24.4
1955	4.9	10.2	48.0
1956	4.8	13.3	36.1
1957	5.9	12.5	47.2
1958	5.0	13.6	36.8
1959	5.0	15.7	31.8
1960	7.6	17.0	44.7
1961	8.0	16.9	47.3
1962	7.6	14.5	52.4
1963	13.4	15.0	89.3
1964	16.3	15.3	106.5
1965	16.5	20.4	80.9
1966	19.0	18.8	101.1
1967	20.1	22.9	87.8
1968	19.8	23.7	83.5
1969	22.1	23.2	95.3
1970	23.8	24.1	98.8
1971	27.6	24.5	112.7
1972	31.6	23.6	133.9
1973	35.0	28.2	124.1
1974	31.5	41.4	76.1
1975	25.3	30.3	83.5
1976	32.2	30.3	106.3
1977	32.3	26.7	121.0
1978	35.2	26.8	131.3
1979	34.9	33.7	103.6
1980	32.9	36.7	89.6

Note:
1. NNP = Net National Product.
Source: Directorate-General of Budget, Accounting and Statistics, Executive Yuan, *National Income of the Republic of China* (1980).

high. Since 1967 the savings ratio has exceeded 20 percent of national income; in the 1970s it was around 30 percent. Such a high savings rate comes mostly from the private sector; however, government savings also contributed to that high ratio. The high government savings ratio in the past seven years accounted for about one-third of domestic savings and was a major financial source of public investment.

Almost half the investment before 1962 was financed by U.S. aid. Almost no private foreign capital flowed into Taiwan before 1961. The situation changed after 1964. Basically, the economy has been able since then to finance its investment by its domestic savings. During the periods 1971–73 and 1976–79, because of great trade surpluses, domestic savings even outweighed investments. That is, part of domestic savings was not utilized within the country. In short, after the take off, the economy moved into a situation of sustained growth.

Investment by the private sector accounted for about half of total investments throughout the period; investment by government-owned public enterprises accounted for about 40 percent of total domestic investment; and the remaining 10 percent was government investment. After 1975, the government greatly intensified the construction of infrastructure and heavier industries, such as transportation, nuclear power generation, petrochemicals, and steel. Because of this intensification, the share of investment by the government and public enterprises went up to 61 percent during the period from 1975 to 1978, although this share was reduced to 52 percent in 1979.

Foreign Investment

Private foreign investment flowed into Taiwan after 1960 (particularly after 1964), most of it going into manufacturing. Private foreign investments approved during the period 1962–69 came to US$378 million. However, the amount that actually reached the manufacturing industry was US$100 million, 5.56 percent of the gross investment in manufacturing during the period.

Foreign investment funds were fairly important, but their

significance varied from year to year. Foreign investment as a percentage of total investment in each sector differed greatly, as is shown in Table 2.13. Some industries received a large proportion of foreign capital inflow. For instance, 40 percent of foreign funds went to the chemical industry in 1962 and 55 percent in 1963. In 1965, 40 percent went to the electrical machinery industry. These two, plus the textile industry, accounted for 67.4 percent of foreign investment for the period 1962–69.

For the period 1973–79, the data are available only for approved foreign investment, not for investment actually received. Approved foreign investment, which was about US$150 million every year in the 1970s, increased to US$330 million in 1979 and US$466 million in 1980. The private foreign investment on approved basis comprised 8 percent of manufacturing investment in 1980.

During the period 1973–79, slightly less than half of foreign investment went into the electrical machinery industry. Chemicals and nonmetallic mineral products received about 27 percent. The industries that had the largest share of foreign investment in a particular industry were electrical machinery (33.6 percent), machinery (22.8 percent), nonmetallic mineral products (20.2 percent), and rubber and petroleum (15.9 percent). The contributions of foreign investment were not only financial, but also extended to better technical know-how and opportunities to import supplies and increase exports.[6]

Income Distribution

As is widely known, raising national income to improve the standard of living is one of the most important goals of economic development. If economic growth leads to greater inequality in income distribution and widens the increasing gap between the rich and the poor, not only is the general public prevented from sharing the fruits of economic development, but social unrest and urban crisis can ensue. The ultimate objective of each country's efforts is, therefore, the more equitable distribution of income. According to the findings of Professor S. Kuznets's empirical study,[7] the twin goals of equity and growth, at least in the early stages of development, are mutually exclusive: As growth ensues, rich and poor tend to become more disparate. However, in the study of Professor Chenery et al.,[8] in which sixty-six countries are compared, the Republic of China is identified as one country that has been able to make considerable progress toward narrowing the income gap while undergoing rapid economic growth.

Economists have traditionally focused much of their attention on the functional distribution of income, related to the determination of the prices of production factors and the shares of production factors in use. Although distribution of family income has by no means been totally neglected, it is probably fair to say that it has been viewed more as a descriptive device that has, until quite recently, not been integrated with the main body of analytical economics. However, the real objective of distributive justice is more usefully conceived of as accelerating the development of poorer groups in society; therefore, a grouping of households according to family income provides more insight into the nature of income distribution.

In the 1950s, Taiwan's family distribution of income was not very different from the unfavorable levels present in most LDCs in their early years of transition, but it improved substantially during the next two decades of rapid growth (see Table 2.14). During the period 1964–79, the income share of the poorest 20 percent of families increased from 7.7 percent to 8.6 percent, while the income share of the richest 20 percent of families decreased from 41.1 percent to 37.5 percent.

As shown in Table 2.15, even when per capita GNP was as low as US$202 in 1964, the income of the two-fifths of the population in the lowest income bracket already amounted to 20.3 percent of the total national income. This was the highest percentage found by Chenery et al. in any of the countries studied by them with a per capita income of less than US$300. By 1972 the same segment of the population was earning 21.9 percent of the total national income.

Table 2.13   Percentage of Foreign Investment

Industry	1962-1969	
	Distribution of Foreign Investment among Industries (based on the amount approved)	Share of Foreign Investment in a Particular Industry (based on the amount actually received)
Food processing	4.7	1.5
Textiles	20.9	4.3
Footwear and others	5.5	5.1
Wood and products	0.9	1.0
Paper and products	1.6	2.7
Leather	0.1	1.5
Rubber and petroleum	4.5	14.5
Chemicals	12.9	4.5
Nonmetallic mineral products	2.0	1.1
Basic metals	6.5	5.5
Machinery	6.8	11.6
Electrical machinery	33.6	18.9
Manufacturing	100.0	—

Sources: Directorate-General of Budget, Accounting and Statistics, Executive Yuan, *National Income of the Republic of China* (1979); Investment Commission, Ministry of Economic Affairs, *Monthly Statistics on Overseas Chinese and Foreign*

1973-1979			
Amount of Foreign Investment (millions of US dollars) (based on the amount approved)	Distribution of Foreign Investment among Industries (based on the amount approved)	Share of Foreign Investment in a Particular Industry (based on the amount approved)	Industry
22	2.1	2.9	Food processing
50	4.8	2.2	Textiles
14	1.3	8.0	Footwear and others
14	1.3	3.9	Wood and products
11	1.1	2.8	Paper and products
7	0.7	13.7	Leather
32	3.0	15.9	Rubber and petroleum
157	14.9	6.1	Chemicals
126	12.0	20.2	Nonmetallic mineral products
59	5.6	3.4	Basic metals
92	8.7	22.8	Machinery
469	44.5	33.6	Electrical machinery
1,053	100.0	7.9	Manufacturing

Investment, Technical Cooperation and Outward Investment, December, various years.

Table 2.14   Changes in Income Distribution of Taiwan Area

Five Equal Divisions of Family Numbers (from Lowest Income to Highest Income)	1964	1966	1968	1970	1972
The income share of the poorest 20% of families (%)	7.7	7.9	7.8	8.4	8.6
The income share of the second poorest 20% of families (%)	12.6	12.4	12.2	13.3	13.2
The income share of the third poorest 20% of families (%)	16.6	16.2	16.3	17.1	17.1
The income share of the fourth poorest 20% of families (%)	22.0	22.0	22.3	22.5	22.5
The income share of the richest 20% of families (%)	41.1	41.5	41.4	38.7	38.6
The ratio of the income share of richest 20% to that of poorest 20%	5.3	5.3	5.3	4.6	4.5

Source: Directorate-General of Budget, Accounting and Statistics, Executive Yuan, *Report on the Survey of Personal Income Distribution in Taiwan Area, Republic of China* (1979), pp. 14, 46.

During the period 1964–79, real family income showed a considerable increase in all income brackets. The rate of increase in family income was greatest for those in the poorest income bracket and smallest for those in the richest income bracket (see Table 2.16).

1974	1976	1978	1979	Five Equal Divisions of Family Numbers (from Lowest Income to Highest Income)
8.8	8.9	8.9	8.6	The income share of the poorest 20% of families
13.5	13.6	13.7	13.7	The income share of the second poorest 20% of families
17.0	17.5	17.5	17.5	The income share of the third poorest 20% of families
22.1	22.7	22.7	22.7	The income share of the fourth poorest 20% of families
38.6	37.3	37.2	37.5	The income share of the richest 20% of families
4.4	4.2	4.2	4.4	The ratio of the income share of richest 20% to that of poorest 20%

Some Other Social and Economic Features

In recent years, social goals as components of social welfare have been the subject of increasing worldwide concern. It has been recognized that the traditional measure of national economic progress – the growth rates of GNP and

Table 2.15 Patterns of Income Distribution in Selected Countries

Country	Year of Data	GNP per Capita (US$)	Relative Shares of Income by Income Class (%)		
			Lowest 40% of All House-holds	Middle 40% of All House-holds	Top 20% of All House-holds
High Inequality					
Philippines	1971	239	11.6	34.6	53.8
Malaysia	1970	330	11.6	32.4	56.0
Brazil	1970	390	10.0	28.4	61.6
South Africa	1965	669	6.2	35.8	58.0
Moderate Inequality					
Burma	1958	82	16.5	38.7	44.8
India	1964	99	16.0	32.0	52.0
Netherlands	1967	1,990	13.6	37.9	48.5
Germany, Fed. Rep.	1964	2,144	15.4	31.7	52.9
Sweden	1963	2,949	14.0	42.0	44.0
Low Inequality					
Rep. of China (Taiwan)	1964	202	20.3	38.6	41.1
Rep. of China (Taiwan)	1972	519	21.9	39.5	38.6
Rep. of China (Taiwan)	1979	1,869	22.3	40.2	37.5
Korea	1970	235	18.0	37.0	45.0
Spain	1965	750	17.6	36.7	45.7
Japan	1963	950	20.7	39.3	40.0
United Kingdom	1968	2,015	18.8	42.2	39.0
Canada	1965	2,920	20.0	39.8	40.2
United States	1970	4,850	19.7	41.5	38.8

Sources: H. Chenery, M.S. Ahluwalia, C.L.G. Bell, J.H. Duloy and R. Jolly, *Redistribution with Growth* (London: Oxford University Press, 1974), pp. 8-9; Directorate-General of Budget, Accounting and Statistics, Executive Yuan, *Report on the Survey of Personal Income Distribution in Taiwan Area, Republic of China* (1979), pp. 14, 46.

per capita income—cannot alone measure real human welfare. As development strategies have shifted their emphasis toward addressing social goals, there has been a growing recognition of the need to devise some indicators that more effectively identify those goals and measure the degree of progress. But one set of important issues concerns the definition of social welfare.

Typical economic and social goals contained in a social welfare system can be identified as these: increased level of per capita income, full employment, price stability, equal income distribution, alleviation of poverty, improvement in the living environment, freedom from disease, social mobility, the achievement of public order and safety, learning and art, and so on. The mutual influences among those goals are obvious. For example, a high rate of income growth will bring about a high rate of employment; however, increased productivity may at the same time generate greater pollution. Furthermore, whether equity advances with economic growth is not yet clear.

At present, there are two kinds of measurement of social welfare, one expressed in terms of money, the other in nonmonetary terms. The "measure of economic welfare" constructed by Professors Nordhaus and Tobin, called "net economic welfare" by Professor Samuelson, and the "net national welfare" (NNW) compiled by the NNW measurement committee of the Economic Council of Japan belong to the first category.[9] They are attempts to establish new indicators of economic welfare by modifying present national income concepts through adding and subtracting positive or negative factors measured in monetary terms.

The other set of measures is expressed in the form of social indicators. Social indicators are designed to measure the state of people's welfare systematically and comprehensively, centering on nonmonetary indicators. Numerous studies and trial calculations have already been made by governments and research organizations of various nations, as well as by such institutional agencies as the United Nations and the Organisation for Economic Co-operation and Development (OECD). The system of social indicators

Table 2.16   Changes in Real Household Income

Five Equal Divisions of Family Numbers (from Lowest to Highest Income)	Rate of Increase During the Period 1964-1979 (%)
The poorest 20% of families	231
The second poorest 20% of families	223
The third poorest 20% of families	213
The fourth poorest 20% of families	208
The richest 20% of families	181

Source: Department of Budget, Accounting and Statistics, Taiwan Provincial Government, *Report on the Survey of Family Income and Expenditure, Taiwan Province, Republic of China*, vol. 1, summary analysis (1979).

often contains some welfare goal areas, such as the environment, health, education, leisure, and so on. The system of social indicators often is in a pyramid shape, logically piled up from some hundreds of indicators to a few goal areas. No matter whether social welfare is expressed in monetary or nonmonetary terms, social welfare, by nature, cannot be free of subjective value judgment.

With these considerations of social welfare measurement in mind, we would like in this section to report on some other social and economic features that have not been discussed in previous sections. Some social indicators of education, sanitation, transportation and communication, housing, and electrification are presented in Table 2.17.

Although some education was available to the people of Taiwan when the island was under Japanese occupation, it was usually limited to the primary level. Advanced education was rare and almost always limited to medical science. After Taiwan was restored to Chinese sovereignty, the government of the Republic of China made an effort to promote education. Not only was a large portion of government money spent on education, but equal opportunity for education was also emphasized. As a result, the level and rate of education increased greatly.

The illiteracy rate of persons 6 years old and older decreased from 55 percent in 1946 to 11.2 percent in 1978. Over the same period, the percentage of school-age children in primary schools increased from 78.6 percent to 99.6 percent. In 1968 nine years of education was made compulsory; this policy has been gradually implemented since then. Over the period 1966–78, the percentage of junior high–age youth (12–14 years old) in junior high schools increased from 48.3 percent to 89.8 percent; the percentage of senior high–age youth (15–17 years old) in senior high and vocational schools increased from 28.3 percent to 51.8 percent; and the percentage of junior college- and university–age youth (18–21 years old) in colleges and universities increased from 11.3 percent to 25.5 percent. The promotion of education on the island greatly contributed to the rapid growth of the economy by providing higher-quality labor for advanced production.

The crude death rate and life expectancy are considered to be two typical indicators of the level of sanitation. The crude death rate in Taiwan decreased from 9.9 per thousand in 1952 to 4.7 per thousand in 1979, and life expectancy increased from 58.6 years to 70.7 years over the same period. Over the same time, the per capita daily calorie intake increased from 2,078 calories to 2,845 calories, and per capita protein intake increased from 49 grams to 79 grams.

Transportation in Taiwan has met with increasing difficulties because land on the island is limited and population is very dense. Particularly in the 1960s, the speed of industrialization greatly exceeded the speed of construction of highways and harbors. However, construction for transportation was intensified during 1975–78. Transportation has been greatly facilitated since then, although the situation is still far from satisfactory. The number of automobiles, motorcyles, and telephones also increased rapidly as the economy grew.

Housing construction during the past three decades has been quite successful. About 90 percent of the houses in

Table 2.17   Social Welfare Indicators of the Republic of China

Item		
1. Education		**1978**
Illiteracy rate (of population 6 years old and older) (percent)	55.0 (1946)	11.2
Percentage of school age children (6-11) in primary schools	78.6 (1946)	99.6
Percentage of junior high age youths (12-14) in junior high schools	48.3 (1966)	89.8
Percentage of senior high age youths (15-17) in senior high and vocational schools	28.3 (1966)	51.8
Percentage of junior college and university age youths (18-21) in junior colleges and universities	11.3 (1966)	25.5
2. Sanitation	**1952**	**1979**
Crude death rate (per 1,000)	9.9	4.7
Life expectancy (years)	58.6	70.7
Per capita daily calorie intake	2,078	2,845
Per capita daily protein intake (grams)	49	79
3. Transportation and Communication	**1952**	**1979**
Automobiles (per 1,000 households)	5	158
Motorcycles (per 1,000 households)	1	926
Telephone (per 1,000 households)	20	713
Correspondence posted per capita	7	50

Table 2.17   Social Welfare Indicators of the Republic of China
(continued)

Item		
4. Housing	**1949**	**1979**
Percentage of households served with electric lighting	33.0	99.7
Percentage of households served with piped water	14.4	63.8
Living space per head (square meter)	4.6	16.9
Dwellings investment/GNP (percent)	1.0 (1952)	3.6
5. Modern Facilities (per 1,000 households)		**1979**
Televisions		1,007
Refrigerators		905
Air conditioners		133
Electric fans		1,762
Washing machines		604
Gas geysers		440
Gas stoves		985
Electric cookers		961
Exhaust fans		387
Mixers		304
Vacuum cleaners		35
Flush toilets		648
Enamelled baths		559
Sewing machines		520

Table 2.17   Social Welfare Indicators of the Republic of China
(continued)

Item	
Cameras	239
Pianos	37
Newspapers	586
Magazines	104

Sources: Council for Economic Planning and Development, Executive Yuan, *Economic Development, Taiwan, Republic of China* (July 1977 and May 1980); Manpower Planning Committee, Council for Economic Planning and Development, Executive Yuan, *Social Welfare Indicators, Republic of China* (1980); Directorate-General of Budget, Accounting and Statistics, Executive Yuan, *Statistical Abstract* (1980); Directorate-General of Budget, Accounting and Statistics, Executive Yuan, *National Income of the Republic of China*(1980); Directorate-General of Budget, Accounting and Statistics, Executive Yuan, *Report on the Survey of Personal Income Distribution in Taiwan Area, Republic of China* (1979).

Taipei City and 80 percent of the houses in Taiwan Province were built after World War II. Living space per head increased from 4.6 square meters in 1949 to 16.9 square meters in 1979. The share of dwelling investment in GNP increased from 1 percent in 1952 to 3.6 percent in 1979.

The rising standard of living is particularly reflected in the more extensive use of modern facilities. In 1979 there were 1,007 television sets per 1,000 households. Refrigerators, gas stoves, washing machines, flush toilets, and the like also became quite common facilities. These are tangible evidence of the improved standard of living throughout the country, which is the ultimate purpose of economic development.

3
Growth, Distribution, and Government Policies, 1953–64

Despite considerable wartime destruction, the physical and institutional infrastructure established under colonial rule in Taiwan was instrumental in the rapid growth of agriculture during the 1950s. The irrigation system, which extended over more than half of Taiwan's cultivated area, proved valuable in ensuring the equitable distribution of the benefits of green-revolution technology. Linkages between agriculture and the rural-based food processing industry led to a marked spatial dispersion of economic growth. This pattern later made possible the provision of substantial nonagricultural employment to farmers. Progress in public health and education during the colonial period provided the basis for a highly productive labor force in both agriculture and industry. In addition, the overwhelmingly Japanese ownership of manufacturing enterprises contributed to a more equal distribution of income in two ways: It reduced the concentration of industrial assets in private Taiwanese hands in the period immediately after World War II, and it provided a source of industrial assets that could be distributed as compensation to landowners under the program of land reform. The preconditions for rapid economic growth and an improved distribution of income thus were considerably more favorable in Taiwan than in the typical developing country.

This chapter probes the reasons for the apparent absence of conflict between growth and equity in Taiwan, especially during the 1950s. Contrary to the experience in most LDCs, the family distribution of income substantially improved during the subphase of primary import substitution in Taiwan.[1] The following sections examine the distribution of assets and the conditions of production during this period, first in agriculture, then to a limited extent in other sectors of the economy. This chapter concludes with a discussion of inferences about the course of income distribution in the 1950s and early 1960s. In subsequent chapters, because of the superior, detailed data available after 1964, we can analyze more rigorously the interplay of economic growth and income distribution during the subphase of export expansion after 1960.

Income Distribution During 1952–64

Information about family distribution of income in Taiwan is meager before 1964, when the Directorate-General of Budget, Accounting, and Statistics (DGBAS) began to conduct regular surveys. One investigator conducted sample surveys of overall income distribution for 1953 and 1959.[2] The Joint Commission on Rural Reconstruction (JCRR) conducted sample surveys of the income of farm families in 1952, 1957, 1962, and 1967.[3] The pattern of overall income distribution for 1953, 1959, and 1964 (see Table 3.1) shows a striking improvement by almost every measure. In 1953 the Gini coefficient, a measure of income inequality (the greater the coefficient, the greater the inequality) was about 0.56, which is comparable to patterns of income distribution now prevailing in Brazil and Mexico. By 1964 the Gini coefficient dropped to 0.33, a level comparable to that of the best performers anywhere.[4] This substantial improvement in overall income distribution during the 1950s can be traced primarily to the rapidly improving rural income distribution and secondarily to the distribution of nonagricultural income, which probably did not worsen and may even have improved slightly.

Table 3.1   Measures of the Equity of Family Distribution
of Income, 1953, 1959, and 1964

Item	1953[a]	1959[b]	1964[c]
Distribution of income by percentile of households (%)			
0—20 (the poorest 20%)	3.0	5.7	7.7
21—40	8.3	9.7	12.6
41—60	9.1	13.9	16.6
61—80	18.2	19.7	22.1
81—95	28.8	26.3	24.8
96—100 (the richest 5%)	32.6	24.7	16.2
Mean income per household (NT$ in 1972 prices)	22,681	31,814	32,452
Per capita GNP in market prices (NT$ in 1972 prices)	6,994	8,629	10,875
Ratio of income share of top 10% to that of bottom 10%	30.40	13.72	8.63
Gini coefficient	0.5580	0.4400	0.3280

a   Data are based on a sample of 301 families, or a sample fraction of 2/1,000.
b   Data are based on a sample of 812 families, or a sample fraction of 4/1,000.
c   Data are based on a sample size of 3,000 families, or a sample fraction of 14.6/ 1,000.

Sources: 1953 from Kowie Chang, "An Estimate of Taiwan Personal Income Distribution in 1953–Pareto's Formula Discussed and Applied," *Journal of Social Science,* vol. 7 (August 1956), p. 260; 1959 from National Taiwan University, College of Law, "Report on Pilot Study of Personal Income and Consumption in Taiwan" (prepared under the sponsorship of a working group of National Income Statistics, DGBAS;processed in Chinese),table A, p. 23; 1964 from DGBAS, *Report on the Survey of Family Income Expenditure, 1964* (Taipei: DGBAS, 1966); Shirley W. Y. Kuo, "Income Distribution by Size in Taiwan Area – Changes and Causes," in *Income Distribution, Employment, and Economic Development in Southeast and East Asia* (Tokyo: Japan Economic Research Center, 1975), vol. 1, pp. 80-146.

Agricultural Development During the 1950s

Land reform alone could not solve the primary constraint facing Taiwan's agriculture: the shortage of land for a rapidly growing agricultural population. Although an ever-increasing number of farmers left agriculture to live and work in Taiwan's expanding urban areas, the population pressure on farmland was severe, especially during the early 1950s. The agricultural population rose from 4.3 million in 1952 to 5.8 million in 1964, an increase of 33 percent. During the same period the total area of cultivated land remained nearly fixed, culminating in a decline in the average size of a family holding from 1.29 hectares to 1.06 hectares. Taiwan overcame these pressures in three ways: by the achievement of substantial increases in agricultural productivity at the intensive margin; by the diversification of agricultural production into more profitable crops; and by the part-time reallocation of labor to nonagricultural activities, including off-farm employment for many members of agricultural families.

The growth of the agricultural sector during the 1950s was impressive. The real net domestic product of agricultural origin increased by about 80 percent during the 1952–64 period, an average rate of 5 percent a year, even though agriculture's share in net domestic product declined from 36 percent to 28 percent. Because the agricultural population increased by only one-third, an agricultural surplus was assured. Although this 5 percent annual increase in net agricultural output during the subphase of import substitution is considerably smaller than that of the industrial sector, it still is an impressive figure by any international standard of comparison. It is even more impressive when two additional factors are considered: The natural fertility of the soil is low, and the land frontier on the mountainous island had essentially been already reached. The growth in agricultural output can only be called dramatic. Between 1952 and 1964 total agricultural production, including forestry, fishing, and livestock, rose by 78 percent; the production of crops alone rose by 59.7 percent. These

Table 3.2   Agricultural Employment, Production, and
Development, 1952–1964

Item	1952	1956	1960	1964
Indexes				
Agricultural population	100.0	110.4	126.2	132.7
Agricultural employment	100.0	100.1	104.7	112.2
Total agricultural production	100.0	121.0	142.8	178.7
Agricultural crop production[a]	100.0	116.8	132.1	159.7
Output of crops and livestock	100.0	121.4	139.1	168.5
Agricultural crop production				
per worker	100.0	115.4	126.1	142.4
Man-days of labor	100.0	104.1	111.5	116.9
Agricultural crop production				
to man-days of labor	100.0	112.2	118.5	136.6
Man-days of labor to				
employment	100.0	104.0	106.5	104.2
Fixed capital	100.0	107.5	116.6	133.6
Working capital	100.0	151.5	169.7	240.2
Multiple cropping	171.9	175.5	183.6	188.0
Diversification[b]	3.54	4.07	4.01	5.75

a   Excludes forestry, fishing, and livestock.
b   The diversification index is calculated for 181 different crops by the formula:
$1/\Sigma$ (value of each product/value of total products)^2.
Sources: Parameters of land and population and indexes of production from Economic
Planning Council, *Taiwan Statistical Data Book, 1975* (Taipei, 1975), pp. 47-51;
indexes of labor man-days, output of crops and livestock, working capital, and
fixed capital from Ho, *Economic Development in Taiwan: 1860-1970* (New Haven:
Yale University Press, 1978), p. 245; index of diversification from Shirley W. Y.
Kuo, "Effects of Land Reform, Agricultural Pricing Policy, and Economic Growth
on Multiple Crop Diversification in Taiwan," in *Economic Essays*, vol. 4 (Taipei:
National Taiwan University, Graduate Institute of Economics, November 1973);
other indexes from calculations by the authors.

production increases were the result primarily of increased
yields of traditional crops, but they were also the result of
the introduction of new crops. The yields of such traditional crops as rice increased 50 percent, but the yields of
relatively new specialty crops, such as cotton and fruits, increased more than 100 percent.[5]

Fixed capital in agriculture expanded by about 34 percent

between 1952 and 1964. Much of this expansion was in irrigation and flood control facilities, which had deteriorated during the war and were rebuilt and expanded during the 1950s. Farm buildings and other structures were added to and improved. The water buffalo was gradually replaced by small tillers and other small mechanical devices. Working capital increased even more dramatically than fixed capital, growing by 140 percent between 1952 and 1964. The continuous introduction of new seed varieties that were responsive to intensive fertilizer applications and the gradual reduction in fertilizer prices and government restrictions enabled Taiwan's total fertilizer use to grow by 91 percent over the same period.[6] As livestock production grew by nearly 120 percent, more and more commercial feeds were imported. Further increases in working capital included widespread use of pesticides, a major postwar innovation that helped to reduce high losses caused by disease and insects.

Taiwan's impressive success in agriculture can be attributed to many factors. Although it is not the purpose of this volume to analyze these factors in detail, nevertheless their relation to the distribution of income is relevant to the argument here. Main factors contributing to the growth and improved income distribution in the agricultural sector are land reform, reorganization of institutional infrastructure, and agricultural pricing policy.

Land Reform

The land reform that the government instituted between 1949 and 1953 was probably the most important factor in improving the distribution of income before the beginning of the subphase of export expansion in the early 1960s.[7] Although much of the reform took place before 1952, the first year for which sample data on the distribution of income exist, it continued to have an impact well into the 1950s. The reform thus remained an important factor in explaining improvements in income distribution during that decade.

Land reform was initiated for several reasons. Although

the Japanese had developed a substantial agricultural infrastructure in Taiwan, they had paid relatively little attention to the distribution of land. Given the large class of tenants, competition for the scarce land was so fierce that the average lease was less than one year. As a result, rents were often equal to 50 percent of the anticipated harvest, especially in the more fertile regions. Contracts frequently were oral; rent payments had to be made in advance; and no adjustments were made for crop failures. These conditions and practices left the typical tenant helpless in any dispute with his landlord. The record of landlord abuse and the need to meet the food demands of postwar Taiwan—which, in addition to its own increased population, included hundreds of thousands of mainland Chinese—laid the groundwork for reform.[8] In addition, the principle of land ownership by the tiller, although it never received much attention, had always been part of the ideology of the Chinese Nationalists. The loss of the mainland and the social unrest threatening in Taiwan made the redistribution of wealth a particularly important issue for the government. Land reform was also considered to be an essential ingredient of agricultural growth and economic recovery. Moreover, it could be imposed by a government that was free of obligations and ties to the landowning class.

The government's conception of land reform was broad. Strengthening farmers' associations and other elements of the organizational and financial infrastructure in rural areas was considered to be important. Moreover, the repair of the physical infrastructure, begun as soon as Taiwan was retroceded to China and almost completed by 1952, increased the effect of land reform on both growth and equity. But the main component of the successful reorganization of the agricultural sector clearly was the three-pronged package of land reform: the program to reduce farm rents, the sale of public lands, and the land-to-the-tiller program.

The first step taken to promote agricultural incentives and output was to reduce farm rents and thereby increase the tenant farmers' share of crop yields. Promulgated in 1949, this program had five basic provisions: First, farm rents could be fixed at no more than 37.5 percent of the anticipated annual yield of the main crops; second, if crops failed because of natural forces, tenant farmers could apply to local farm-tenancy committees for a further reduction; third, tenant farmers no longer had to pay their rent in advance; fourth, written contracts and fixed leases of three to six years had to be registered; and fifth, tenants had the first option to purchase land from its owners. The reform affected about 43 percent of the 660,000 farm families, 75 percent of the 410,000 part-owners and tenants, and 40 percent of the 650,000 hectares of private farmland. Prices of farmland immediately dropped—paddy field prices by 20 percent and dry field prices by more than 40 percent by December 1949 and a further 66 percent by 1952.[9] Equally important, the requirement for written contracts and the fixing of standard reduced rents enabled tenants to benefit from their own increased efforts for the first time. This incentive was a primary ingredient of the sustained increase in Taiwan's agricultural productivity during the early 1950s. With higher yields and lower rents, the average income of tenant farmers rose by 81 percent between 1949 and 1952.[10] These rising incomes enabled tenants to purchase land put up for sale by their landlords; about 6 percent of private farmland changed hands.

Given the success of the program to reduce farm rents, the government decided to accelerate the program initiated in 1948 to sell public land to tenant farmers. About 170,000 hectares of public land that had formerly been owned by the Japanese—about 25 percent of Taiwan's arable land—were suitable for cultivation. Taiwan Sugar Corporation owned most of this land and leased part of it to tenant farmers. The program gave priority in land purchases to cultivators of public land and landless tenants. The size of parcels was limited according to predetermined fertility grades, and the average size was 1 chia (1 chia = 0.97 hectares). Selling prices were 2.5 times the value of the annual yield of the main crops; payments in kind were set to coincide with the harvest season over a ten-year period. In all, 35 percent of

Taiwan's arable public land was sold during 1948–53, and 43 percent during 1953–58.

With the government setting the example of returning l.nd to the tiller, the stage was set for the most dramatic component of the three-pronged package: the compulsory sale of land by landlords. This program stipulated that privately owned land in excess of specified amounts per landowner had to be sold to the government, which would resell that land to tenants.[11] The purchase price was set at 2.5 times the annual yield of the main crops. Landlords were paid 70 percent of the purchase price in land bonds denominated in kind and 30 percent in industrial stock of four public enterprises previously owned by the Japanese. The selling prices and conditions of repayment were the same as for the sale of public lands. This third program had a dual objective. The new owner-cultivators were encouraged to work harder because they would benefit from any increases in agricultural output. The landlords, deprived of the privilege of living comfortably off the land, were encouraged to participate in the industrial development of Taiwan through ownership of four large-scale industrial enterprises. Between May and December of 1953, tenant households acquired 244,000 hectares of farmland, 16.4 percent of the total area cultivated in Taiwan during 1951–55.

Tables 3.3 and 3.4 summarize the extent of land reform and its importance for the redistribution of wealth in Taiwan. Because of the reform, the distribution of landholdings changed dramatically between 1952 and 1960. The rising share of families owning medium-sized plots of land, ranging from 0.5 to 3 chia, reflects this change: Their share increased from 46 percent in 1952 to 76 percent in 1960. The largest rise was in the share of families owning between 0.5 and 1 chia. What is even more dramatic, the average size of holdings in all categories of less than 5 chia increased. The combined share in total land of families owning less than 3 chia increased from 58 percent in 1952 to 85 percent in 1960. The proportion of land cultivated by tenants fell from 44 percent in 1948 to 17 percent in 1959.

Table 3.3   Area and Households Affected by Land Reform,
by Type of Reform

Item	Type of Reform			
	Reduction of Farm Rents	Sale of Public Land	Land-to-the-tiller Program	Total Redistribution[a]
Area affected (thousands of chia)	257	72	194	215
Farm households affected (thousands)	302	140	195	334
Ratio of cultivated area affected to total area[b] (%)	29	8	16	25
Ratio of farm households affected to total farm households (%)	43	20	28	48

a   Comprises land distributed under the sale of public land and the land-to-the-tiller
program.
b   Total area is the total area cultivated in 1951-55.
Note: Figures may not reconcile because of rounding.
Source: Samuel P.S. Ho, *Economic Development in Taiwan: 1860-1970* (New Haven:
Yale University Press, 1978), p. 163.

The proportion of tenant farmers in farm families fell from 38 percent in 1950 to 15 percent in 1960. The ratio of owner-cultivators to total farm families increased from 36 percent in 1949 to 60 percent in 1957. Part-owner farmers and owner-cultivators owned more than 83 percent of the total farm land in 1957.

The incentive to make extra efforts in cultivation was great after land reform. First, after rent reduction, the tenant was able to benefit not only by the reduction in rent, but also by any increase in production beyond the standard production. This was a motivating force in promoting multiple cropping. Second, the superiority of an owner-farmer system over a tenancy system was obvious on a per

Table 3.4 Distribution of Farm Families and Agricultural Land, by Type of Cultivator, Before and After Land Reform

Item	Before Land Reform (1949)		After Land Reform (1957)	
	Number of families	%	Number of families	%
Owner	224,378	36	455,357	60
Tenant	239,939	39	125,653	17
Part-owner	156,558	25	178,224	23
Total	620,875	100	759,234	100

Source: Department of Agriculture & Forestry, Provincial Government of Taiwan, *Taiwan Agricultural Yearbook* (1950, p. 28; 1967, p. 47.)

family, per person, or even per hectare basis. The farm income of the tenant had been only three-fourths of the income of the other two categories. Therefore, a major change in tenancy conditions provided a great incentive to produce more and made possible more efficient utilization of the agricultural labor force.

After the land reform, farmers had a freer choice of crops, because, as owner-cultivators, they were under no obligation to produce rice for rental payment. Thus, the land reform tended to reduce the relative share of rice production and to increase the share of other crops, vegetables, fruits, livestock, and poultry. Moreover, the technological change in agriculture after land reform was largely centered on the intensive use of land with more labor input.

Although the government compensated landlords for the land they were forced to give up, this compensation was only 2.5 times the standard annual yield; market values of land ranged between 5 and 8 times the annual yield. The policy thus represented a substantial redistribution of wealth. The total value of wealth redistributed as a result of this price difference was equivalent to about 13 percent of

Taiwan's gross domestic product in 1952.[12] Furthermore, bonds used to reimburse landowners paid an interest rate of only 4 percent, substantially less than the prevailing market rates. Because of the landlords' lack of experience in nonagricultural matters, most landlords did not place much value on the 30 percent of their compensation received as industrial stocks. They promptly sold the stocks at prices far below value. Most of their proceeds went to consumption; some went to investments in small businesses. The majority of landlords thus ended up being not much better off than the new owner-cultivators.[13]

Through the reduction of rents and the redistribution of assets, the land reform had a marked effect on the functional distribution of income. Between 1941 and 1956 the combined share of property in total agricultural income fell from 63.7 percent to 44.3 percent (see Table 3.5). The sharp reduction in the share of property income was thus accompanied by a broader distribution of that income. Two in-

Table 3.5   Distribution of Agricultural Income, by Factor, 1941—1956

(percent)

Year	Property		Labor
	Land	Capital	
Before land reform			
1941	52.2	11.5	36.3
1942	52.0	11.4	36.6
1943	45.7	10.0	44.3
After land reform			
1953	37.4	8.2	54.4
1954	38.1	8.4	53.5
1955	38.2	8.4	53.4
1956	36.3	8.0	55.7

Source: S. C. Hsieh and T. H. Lee, "Agricultural Development and Its Contributions to Economic Growth in Taiwan," *Economic Digest Series*, no. 17 (Taipei: JCRR, 1966).

vestigators have estimated the shares of farm income by type of recipient before the land reform, using the 1936–40 average, and after the land reform, using the 1956–60 average.[14] According to these estimates, the cultivators' share of farm income increased from 67 percent to 82 percent; the share of government and public institutions, which received repayments from new landowners, increased from 8 percent to 12 percent; but the share of landlords and moneylenders declined from 25 percent to 6 percent.

Reorganization of the Institutional Infrastructure

The institutional infrastructure of Taiwan's agriculture was extensively reorganized and improved during the 1950s. The farmers' associations and credit cooperatives, set up by the Japanese to facilitate agricultural extension programs and rice procurement, were top-down institutions dominated by landlords and nonfarmers. As a result, most farmers did not directly benefit from them. In 1952, the government consolidated those institutions in multipurpose farmers' associations restricted to farmers and serving their interests. In addition to the original function of agricultural extension, the activities of farmers' associations expanded to include a credit department, which accepted deposits from farmers and made loans to them, and to provide facilities for purchasing, marketing, warehousing, and processing agricultural produce.[15] The associations thus became clearinghouses for farmers, who controlled and maintained them and viewed them as their own creatures.

The other major institutional reform affecting agriculture during the 1950s was the establishment of the Joint Commission on Rural Reconstruction (JCRR) by the U.S. Congress in 1948. Its main functions were to allocate U.S. aid, to provide technical assistance, and to help the government plan and coordinate programs for agricultural extension, research, and experimentation. Thus, although the farmers' associations provided the much-needed organizational structure at local levels and facilitated the efficient flow of agricultural surpluses to the industrial sector, the JCRR was a major catalyst. It funded and initiated many new farming techniques, and it introduced new crops and new markets. For example, the JCRR was behind the introduction of asparagus and mushroom cultivation, which led to the highly successful production and export performance of those commodities in the 1950s.

Technological change, introduced mainly by such government-supported research agencies as the JCRR, clearly was a significant factor in generating the increased agricultural output.[16] In 1960 Taiwan had 79 agricultural research workers for every 100,000 persons active in agriculture, compared with 60 in Japan, 4.7 in Thailand, 1.6 in the Philippines, and 1.2 in India.[17] The research agencies successfully introduced new strains of rice and sugar and such new crops as asparagus and mushrooms, as well as pesticides, insecticides, and new agricultural tools and machinery. In the Hayami-Ruttan terminology, most of the technological change was of the chemical variety, not the mechanical.[18]

Agricultural Pricing Policy

The agricultural pricing policies were implemented mainly through the following actions. First, by various methods of compulsory rice collection, the government controlled the supply of rice and kept a large part of rice consumption from going through the market mechanism. Thus, it contributed to the stabilization of the price of rice. Second, through collection of land tax in kind, the rice fertilizer barter system, and the purchase and collection of rice at a price relatively lower than the market price, the government made huge profits from the rice collection operation. These profits are really a form of "hidden rice tax." Third, by offering guaranteed prices for sugar cane, corn, mushrooms, asparagus, and so on, the government encouraged the production of crops other than rice.

Thus, as a result of the agricultural pricing policies, rice production underwent a relative decline and other higher-value agricultural products increased instead (see Tables 3.6 and 3.7). This change of agricultural structure and intense

Table 3.6   Share of Rice in Agricultural Products

(percent)

Year	Rice	Agricultural Products Other Than Rice	Ratio of Rice to the Agricultural Products Other Than Rice
1952	50.2	49.8	100.8
1955	45.9	54.1	84.8
1960	45.5	54.5	83.5
1965	36.8	63.2	58.2
1970	31.7	68.3	46.4
1975	34.0	66.0	51.5
1979	26.8	73.2	36.6

Source: Department of Agriculture and Forestry, Taiwan Provincial Government, *Taiwan Agricultural Year Book,* various years.

Table 3.7   Change in Agricultural Structure

(percent)

Year	Common Crops	Special Crops	Fruits	Vege- tables	Live- stock	Common Crops and Special Crops	High Value Agricultural Products
1952	61.6	16.9	3.0	4.1	14.4	78.5	21.5
1955	57.5	17.1	2.6	4.1	18.7	74.6	25.4
1960	58.1	13.9	3.3	4.5	20.2	72.0	28.0
1965	47.0	13.8	8.5	6.1	24.6	60.8	39.2
1970	40.7	10.1	8.3	11.3	29.6	50.8	49.2
1975	40.1	14.0	5.8	10.0	30.1	54.1	45.9
1979	31.5	8.0	9.2	14.4	36.9	39.5	60.5

Source: Same as Table 3.6.

agricultural diversification provided a fundamental basis for the development of food processing manufacturing and export expansion in the 1960s.

Given the physical and organizational improvement of the environmental infrastructure and the pervasive package of land reform, farmers had the incentives and the tools to improve their situation during the subphase of primary import substitution, during which government policies usually discriminate against agriculture. Moreover, the technological change seemed to be of a type that generally used labor and saved land and capital. Although the number of persons employed in agriculture increased by 12 percent between 1952 and 1964, the number of man-days increased by 17 percent. Consequently, the number of working days per worker steadily increased. In 1965 the average worker had 156 days of farm employment, compared with 90 days in 1946 and 134 days in 1952.[19] As a result, the number of working days per hectare of land increased from approximately 170 in 1948–50 to about 260 in 1963–65.[20]

Larger labor inputs to the cultivation of traditional crops and the diversification into new crops resulted in more intensive cultivation of land. Between 1952 and 1964 the multiple-cropping index increased from 172 to 188; the diversification index increased from 3.54 to 5.75 (see Figure 3.1). The shift toward such labor-intensive crops as vegetables and away from the complete dominance of the traditional crops of rice and sugar was continuous. As an indication of the labor intensity of vegetable cultivation, the cultivation of one hectare of asparagus requires 2,900 times the labor input of the cultivation of one hectare of rice.

Despite the substantial increase in the absorption of labor in agriculture between 1952 and 1964, rural underemployment continued during the 1950s and has been estimated to be about 40 percent during that decade.[21] The smaller, poorer farms were especially unable to generate sufficient income or to keep the entire family fully employed. This pattern led to a small amount of net physical migration out of the agricultural sector, estimated at less than 1 percent annually during the 1950s. Mostly, however, farmers in-

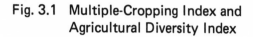

Fig. 3.1   Multiple-Cropping Index and
Agricultural Diversity Index

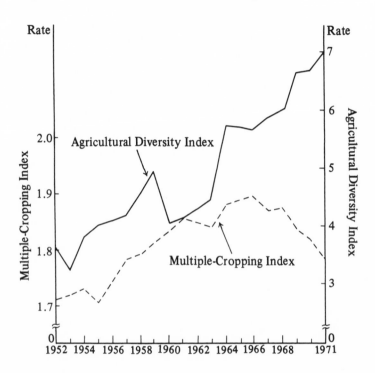

Note:

$$\text{Diversity index} = \cfrac{1}{\Sigma \left(\cfrac{\text{value of each product}}{\text{value of total product}}\right)^2} = \cfrac{1}{\underset{i}{\Sigma} \left(\cfrac{y_i}{Y}\right)^2}$$

$$\text{multiple-cropping index} = \frac{\text{cropping area}}{\text{cultivated area}} \times 100$$

For details, please see: Shirley W.Y. Kuo, "Effects of Land Reform, Agricultural Pricing Policy and Economic Growth on Multiple-Crop Diversification in Taiwan," special issue on Multiple-Cropping in Asian Development, *The Philippine Economic Journal,* vol. 14, nos. 1 and 2 (1975).

Table 3.8   Distribution of Industrial Production, by Public and Private Ownership, 1952—1964

(percent)

Year	Total		Manufacturing	
	Public	Private	Public	Private
1952	56.6	43.4	56.2	43.8
1953	55.9	44.1	55.9	44.1
1954	52.7	47.3	49.7	50.3
1955	51.1	48.9	48.7	51.3
1956	51.0	49.0	48.3	51.7
1957	51.3	48.7	48.7	51.3
1958	50.0	50.0	47.2	52.8
1959	48.7	51.3	45.2	54.8
1960	47.9	52.1	43.8	56.2
1961	48.2	51.8	45.3	54.7
1962	46.2	53.8	42.3	57.7
1963	44.8	55.2	40.6	59.4
1964	43.7	56.3	38.9	61.1

Source: Economic Planning Council, *Taiwan Statistical Data Book, 1975*, p. 75.

creasingly sought off-farm employment in the rapidly growing rural industrial sector. Consequently, underemployment did not develop into as serious a problem as it has in most other LDCs.[22] The pattern of agricultural growth and the participation in that growth by rich and poor farmers were the basic ingredients of the dramatic improvement in the distribution of income in Taiwan during the 1950s.

The Distribution of Assets and Industrial Growth

What can be said about the distribution of assets outside agriculture during this period? Obviously much less, but broad patterns, nevertheless, are indicative. The 56.6 percent share of the public sector in industrial output in 1952

Mining		Electricity, Gas, and Water	Year
Public	Private	Public	
28.3	71.7	100.0	1952
24.4	75.6	100.0	1953
32.5	67.5	100.0	1954
28.5	71.5	100.0	1955
26.5	73.5	100.0	1956
26.3	73.7	100.0	1957
24.2	75.8	100.0	1958
22.6	77.4	100.0	1959
24.2	75.8	100.0	1960
18.8	81.2	99.9	1961
19.6	80.4	99.6	1962
19.1	80.9	99.7	1963
20.5	79.5	99.8	1964

characterized the Taiwan economy in the early 1950s (see Table 3.8). This pattern was mainly a consequence of the Chinese takeover of Japanese assets at the end of World War II. In addition, before the movement of the central government from the mainland, the government dismantled and shipped industrial equipment, such as textile spindles, and in some cases, entire enterprises to Taiwan. Firms under public ownership were initially plagued with typical problems: inefficiency, overstaffing, rigid pay structures, and bureaucratic interference. Meanwhile, small firms and simple equipment characterized the private sector. As late as 1961, 31 percent of all manufacturing establishments employed fewer than ten workers.[23] All industry was hampered by the shortage of foreign exchange.[24]

This situation was undoubtedly favorable to the equity of the initial distribution of industrial assets. Because private ownership of capital did not exist on a large scale, entrepreneurs generally were not in a position to gain monopolistic control of industries or to accumulate great wealth from property income. In the private sector the small size and labor intensity of firms were favorable to the share of workers. Profits of the larger, more capital-intensive firms went to the government, not to private entrepreneurs.

During the early 1950s, the government began transferring the four public enterprises under its control to private ownership: Taiwan Cement Corporation, Taiwan Pulp and Paper Corporation, Taiwan Industrial and Mining Corporation, and Taiwan Agriculture and Forestry Development Corporation. This transfer was not easily accomplished. The government had difficulty finding buyers because of the lack of accumulated private wealth and entrepreneurial expertise and because of the poor track records of these enterprises. In 1953 a large portion of government assets was, nevertheless, transferred as partial payment to landlords under the land-to-the-tiller program. As a result of this transfer and such other factors as the increasingly rapid growth of private industry, the government-owned share of total industrial production fell to 43.7 percent in 1964. Industries remaining in the public sector included utilities, railroads, shipbuilding, and iron and steel. Thus, despite the substantial drop in government ownership, the public control of assets continued to be important. This was particularly true in the most capital-intensive industries, in which growth is least favorable to the distribution of income.

Taiwan's industrial growth during 1952–64 was impressive: net domestic product (NDP) grew at an average annual rate of 7 percent, the industrial sector at an average annual rate of 11 percent. By 1964 the real NDP of the industrial sector was more than 250 percent higher than in 1952; that sector's share of total NDP rose from 18 percent to 28 percent. Most of this growth was the result of the emergence of the manufacturing subsector: Its share in NDP grew from only 11 percent in 1952 to more than 20 percent in 1964.[25] The concentration on food processing and textiles, as well as on other industries that typically predominate during the subphase of primary import substitution, continued to be heavy.

The reorientation of industrial output between the late 1950s and early 1960s is also reflected in the changing composition of imports and exports. Although total imports in constant prices more than doubled during the 1952–64 period, the share of imports of consumption goods in total imports rapidly declined from 20 percent to 6 percent. In constant prices those imports in 1964 were slightly below their 1952 level. Imports of raw materials for agriculture and industry kept pace with the growth of total imports. But imports of capital goods, such as machinery and electrical and transport equipment, almost quadrupled. This growth reflected the twin efforts to shift industrial activity away from the narrow domestic market toward wider international markets and to provide the physical infrastructure needed for that shift. Even though government policy was to reduce imports in the 1950s, total imports doubled during 1952–64. This expansion reflected the need to fuel import substitution during the 1950s, as is evidenced by the growth of imports of capital goods by about 20 percent per year before 1960.[26] Imports of raw materials, which were growing steadily at 8 percent per year during the 1950s, started to grow at 11 percent per year in response to the new opportunities of the export-substitution era. This policy of accelerated imports of raw materials, combined with the use of unskilled labor, was at the heart of the drive that followed for expanding labor-intensive industrial exports.

As would be expected in any developing economy, imports continued to outstrip exports throughout the 1952–64 period in Taiwan. Nevertheless, exports in constant prices quadrupled. Moreover, industrial exports increased by a phenomenal 2,800 percent and dramatically changed the composition of exports. The share in total exports of agricultural and related exports declined from 92 percent to less than 60 percent in only twelve years; the share of industrial exports went up fivefold, from 8 percent to 40 percent. Industrial production and export growth during this period were concentrated in the textile, leather, and wood and paper industries. Most of the increase occurred between 1960 and 1964, that is, after changes in policies and factor endowment ushered in the subphase of export expansion.

Monetary Policies in the 1950s

Stabilization Policies

Immediately after the war the most urgently needed policy for overall growth was price stabilization, because during the period 1946–48, prices had risen at an annual rate of about 500 percent and then accelerated to about 3,000 percent in the first half of 1949. Stabilization policies were implemented through various measures, among which monetary reform was essential.

Monetary Reform. The New Taiwan Dollar Reform was put into effect on June 15, 1949, amid rampant hyperinflation. The old currency was devalued by a factor of 40,000, the most conservative full reserve system was adopted, and the limitation on issuance was strictly enforced. Speculation in gold was strictly prohibited, and the government sold gold periodically. This mechanism stabilized the price of gold on the one hand and absorbed money supply on the other.

Right after the monetary reform, the inflation rate slowed down and prices only tripled in 1950. Compared with the 3,000 percent increase experienced in the first half in 1949, this was a great success. Inflation was more controlled after 1951, and the annual increase in prices was 8.8 percent during 1952–60 before it declined to 3 percent in 1961 and afterwards. Although it took twelve years to accomplish this, the contribution of the monetary reform to price stabilization and economic development was great.

Interest Rate Policy. Another important measure promoting stabilization was the introduction of preferential interest savings deposits in March 1950. Because of the then-prevailing hyperinflation, the duration of the deposits was very short—only one month at the outset. Longer-term deposits were added later as price stability was achieved, and the amount of deposits gradually increased.

The principal characteristic of the preferential interest savings deposits was their high interest rate. At that time, the yearly interest rate for one-year time deposits was 20 percent. The interest rate of these new deposits was 7 percent per month, which, if compounded, would amount to 125 percent per year. Although the interest rate was actually still below the inflation rate in 1950, setting such a high interest rate required intelligence and determination on the part of the government.

The preferential interest savings deposits were very effective. At the beginning of 1950, time deposits in all banks amounted to only NT$2 million. After the inauguration of the preferential interest deposits, the amount increased to NT$35 million in eight months, making up about 7 percent of the money supply. The interest rate was lowered from 7 percent per month to 3.5 percent and again to 3 percent in 1950; but when a decrease in deposits was observed, the interest rate was raised to 4.2 percent. The interest rate was gradually reduced to 2 percent in November 1952, at which time preferential interest savings deposits accounted for 44 percent of the money supply. After 1953 the government began providing preferential interest savings deposits for longer terms. The number of accounts on these longer terms gradually increased.

On March 5, 1956, the authorities started a new kind of time deposit that matured in six months or one year and could not be mortgaged, bearing monthly interest rates of 1.5 percent and 1.8 percent, respectively. These rates were higher than those for the deposits that could be accepted as security for loans, the interest of the latter having been reduced to 0.85 percent and 1 percent, respectively, for deposits in one-month and three-month accounts. Because of the reduction in the interest rates for shorter-term deposits, all deposits tended to be of longer maturity. At the end of 1956, deposits in one-year accounts comprised 27 percent of the total deposits.

On July 16, 1957, the Bank of Taiwan began to accept time deposits maturing in two years and at the same time abolished one-month deposits. The interest rate for deposits of three months' duration was further lowered to 0.85 percent; that for deposits of two years' duration was fixed at 1.9 percent. During 1958, the total amount in one-year deposits more than doubled; from mid-1957 to the end of 1958, the amount in six-month deposits nearly doubled.[27]

At the end of 1958, the authorities suspended the preferential interest savings deposits. The total outstanding deposits at that time amounted to NT$1,500 million, or 29 percent of the money supply. For a period of about nine years, from March 1950 to the end of 1958, the financial authorities had relied on these savings deposits as a means to call in a tremendous amount of idle capital from the market, thus contributing greatly to the stability of the island's economy during those years. Meanwhile, the Bank of Taiwan, then functioning as the central bank, succeeded in bringing credit expansion of the commercial banks under its effective control. Extensions of loans to business were carefully coordinated with the overall policies.

The Government Budget. During this period, the authorities concerned spared no effort in doing away with any factor that might bring about economic instability. On the fiscal side, a great effort was made to achieve a balanced budget. A part of U.S. aid was efficiently utilized to supplement the government deficit up until 1961. The government budget, including transfer receipts, actually had a surplus every year, even before 1961, and this provided an important financial source of investment in infrastructure.

The 1950s Foreign Exchange Policy

In 1949, when the monetary reform was put into effect, a

Table 3.9   Foreign Transfers and Government Current Surplus

Year	Foreign Transfers to the Government Sector in Percent of Government Expenditure	Government Current Surplus Net of Foreign Transfers in Percent of Government Expenditure	Government Current Surplus Inclusive of Foreign Transfers in Percent of Government Expenditure	Government Expenditure in Percent of GNP
1951	32.5	−11.3	21.2	17.6
1956	20.8	− 5.2	15.6	20.1
1961	25.2	− 7.2	18.0	19.1
1963	7.6	− 0.2	7.4	18.7
1964	1.8	6.5	8.3	17.5
1965	3.7	10.5	14.2	17.0

Source: Directorate-General of Budget, Accounting and Statistics, Executive Yuan, *National Income of the Republic of China* (1980).

simple exchange rate was adopted: Those exchanging foreign for domestic currency were given part in cash, at the rate of NT$5 to US$1, and the other part in exchange settlement certificates (ESCs) of equivalent value. These ESCs were freely negotiable in the market or could be sold to the Bank of Taiwan at the official rate. For importers, foreign exchange was approved rather liberally, and the ESCs were sold for importation of permissible items at the official rate. However, owing to the great deficit of trade balance and continued inflation, applications for foreign exchange soon outgrew the available supply. The official supply price of ESCs was repeatedly devalued.

In 1951, along with the substantial devaluation, a multiple exchange rate was introduced. Imports of goods by the public sector, and of plants, important raw materials, and intermediate inputs by the private sector, were given a lower official rate; imports of other goods were given a higher ESC rate. The export earnings of sugar, rice, and salt were given a lower ESC rate than private export earnings. After 1951 the exchange rate was overvalued due to continuous inflation, thus hampering exports and encouraging imports and import substitution.

After several devaluations, the foreign exchange system was revised again in November 1958. This time exchange settlement certificates were to apply equally to all kinds of exports and imports. In addition, the price of ESCs was fixed at a level close to that of the market price. The government permitted the Taiwan Sugar Corporation, which was the holder of a huge number of ESCs, to sell them at a price very close to the market price and then, from July 1960 on, let the corporation sell them at a fixed price below the market price. (From August 1960 on, the price of an ESC reflected the official basic foreign exchange rate.) This made the market exchange rate gradually stabilize at the rate of NT$40 to US$1. The high international sugar price in 1963 enabled the company to earn more than enough foreign exchange. Making use of this abundance of foreign exchange, the government abolished the system of ESCs, and the direct exchange settlement of the present system took its place.

Relative Prices of Import Goods and Export Goods

In the early 1950s, the price ratio of import substitutes to export goods went up appreciably. The relative prices of cotton textiles and rice underwent a dramatic change, increasing from 2:1 during 1949–50 to 4–5:1 in 1951–52.[28] This change was of particular significance. Rice was Taiwan's main agricultural product, some of which was exported, and textiles were major imports at that time. Import substitution of textile goods, therefore, received full official blessing.[29] K. Y. Yin, then vice-chairman of the Taiwan Production Board, also emphasized the long-run comparative advantage. He organized a joint textile group to give full support to the expansion of production of cotton yarn fabrics by providing the necessary raw materials to the manufacturing firms through U.S. aid, imports, and allocation of funds.

Some export promotion measures were begun in the early 1950s. In 1954 a system of rebates of import duties on raw materials was introduced. In 1956 a system of utilizing a certain portion of foreign exchange earnings for importing raw materials was initiated. However, overvaluation of the currency and the multiple exchange rate structure still favored import substitution.

An urgent need for foreign exchange earnings and increasingly limited domestic markets soon brought easy import substitution to an end. By 1958 the investment climate was gloomy and a fundamental change in policy was required.

Education

Education was of major concern to the government, and a great deal was spent on it. The expenditure for education, science, and culture consistently accounted for more than 13 percent of the budget at all levels of government during 1954–68, increasing to 18 percent by 1971. Because of the government's emphasis on education, enrollment in the 6–11 age group reached 96 percent in 1961 and 98 percent in 1971, increasing from 80 percent in 1951. The proportion of primary school graduates who went on to junior high school increased from 32 percent in 1951 to 51 percent in 1961 and 80 percent in 1971. The proportion of junior high school graduates who went on to senior high school remained around 72 percent during the twenty-year period. As a high-quality labor force is a necessary condition for effective labor absorption, the government's emphasis on upgrading education contributed in part to labor absorption.

Extensive education generally leads to a higher income. Accordingly, providing equal opportunity for education is an efficient way to achieve a more equal income distribution. Although there is no way to ensure a completely equal education for everyone because of differences in teachers, facilities, and so on, two important government policies in the present education system of the Republic of China have made higher education equally accessible to rich and poor. The first policy is a low tuition system: Average tuition is US$100 a year at public colleges and US$300 at private colleges. The second policy is a unified entrance examination system, by which each student has a fair opportunity for competition. With no discrimination between rich and poor, it is possible for a larger proportion of students from low-income families to be admitted to better colleges.

Labor Intensity

As will be more fully explained in Chapter 5, the pattern of industrial growth can affect the family distribution of income through changes in the functional distribution of income. For example, if the wage share goes up because of the adoption of a labor-intensive growth path, the distribution of income will improve, assuming that wage income is better distributed than property income, which it generally is. If the wage share declines because of technological changes that save labor and increase capital use, the distribution of family income will worsen. Between 1951 and 1954, the early period of import substitution, the share of wage income in total income sharply increased from 40.7 percent to 46.2 percent. In ensuing years that share was fairly stable, at least until the onset of export substitution policies again increased the wage share in the 1960s, especially after commercialization. Given the distortion of relative prices that usually accompanies import substitution, Taiwan's achievement of a stable wage share is significant. The chief reasons for this performance are that prices of factors of production, i.e., capital and labor, were more distorted before 1954 than subsequently and that import substitution policies were relatively mild.

If a stable or improving wage share is one precondition for the improved distribution of nonagricultural income, the adoption of a labor-intensive growth path is another. The data indicate that growth in Taiwan during the 1950s was not focused on highly capital-intensive industries, as is typical of many LDCs. In fact, the most labor-intensive branches of industry grew at rates well above the average. The share in total industrial value added of the seven most labor-intensive industries rose from 10.9 percent in 1954 to 17.6 percent in 1961. The large textile and apparel industry, which still was more labor-intensive than the average for all industry, grew at a slower rate; the tobacco industry, the least labor-intensive, became smaller. In addition, manufacturing in Taiwan was much more labor intensive than in the typical LDC, e.g., Pakistan.

The labor-intensive bias of manufacturing, the good distribution of industrial assets, the pattern of growth and spatial dispersion of the more labor-intensive industries, the relatively mild price distortions—all these factors served to improve the overall distribution of nonagricultural income or at least to prevent its worsening. This performance, together with the rapidly improving rural income distribution, paved the way for the substantial decline observed in overall income inequality during the 1950s. It is not possible to say more than this. The meager quantity and quality of data for the 1950s, especially for factor income, preclude formal decomposition analysis of the type undertaken in subsequent chapters. Instead, the estimates should be viewed as orders of magnitude that might explain the marked tendency for the value of the Gini coefficient to decline between 1953 and 1964. But even if there can be doubt about the size of income distribution levels and changes, there is strong evidence that a substantial improvement occurred during the 1950s. This improvement was the result of an unusually good initial distribution of assets, a relatively mild regime of import substitution, the efficient use of abundant labor, and the early attention to the rural sector. Furthermore, the general liberalization of the economy under the reforms of the early 1960s could only serve to reinforce these trends. A more precise analysis linking growth and income distribution nevertheless had to await the superior data that began to become available in 1964.

4

Economic Policies in the 1960s

The primary objectives of Taiwan's economic policies in the 1960s were export promotion and encouragement of investment in labor-intensive industries. As will be examined in the succeeding chapters, export expansion was a decisive factor in the successful, rapid industrial growth of the 1960s and 1970s.

Rapid development of labor-intensive industries created job opportunities, particularly for unskilled labor. The share of wage income in total income, which consists of both wage income and property income, increased. This was one of the most important factors in achieving rapid growth with improved income distribution in the 1960s in the Republic of China. After Taiwan achieved full employment, a stronger demand for unskilled labor made the wages of unskilled labor increase even faster than the wages of skilled labor. Assuming that unskilled labor comes mostly from relatively low-income families, we can thus identify labor-intensive, export-promoting economic policies as being crucial to the success of improved income distribution during rapid industrialization. Therefore, in this chapter economic policies for export promotion and encouragement of investment in the 1960s will be briefly reviewed.

Nineteen-Point Economic Financial Reform

In the early 1950s, economic policies favored import substitution. But as domestic markets became increasingly limited and the need for foreign exchange earnings grew urgent, new policies favoring export expansion were required. Policy changes were made in 1956 and 1960. An optimistic growth target of 8 percent for the period 1961 to 1964 was set in the Third Four-Year Plan, which also introduced the Nineteen-Point Economic Financial Reform. Its basic objectives were

1. to make a thorough review of past control measures in order to liberalize those measures;
2. to give preferential treatment to private businesses in regard to taxes, foreign exchange, and financing;
3. to reform the tax system and its administration to enhance capital formation;
4. to reform foreign exchange and trade systems, aiming at the establishment of a unified exchange rate and liberalization of trade control, consistent with the payments situation; and
5. to promote measures encouraging export expansion, improve procedures governing the settlement of foreign exchange earned by exporters, and increase contacts with foreign business organizations.

Other measures were also taken, based on the essential spirit of this Nineteen-Point Economic Financial Reform, the most important of which will be explained below.

Investment Incentives

The Statute for Encouragement of Investment was enacted pursuant to the nineteen-point reform measures. The main purposes of this statute were to facilitate the acquisition of plant sites and to provide production incentives through tax exemptions and deductions. The salient points of the Statute for Encouragement of Investment may be given as follows:

1. Income tax holiday: The strongest production incentive is the "five-year tax holiday" set forth in Article 5,

whereby a productive enterprise conforming to the statute's criteria is exempt from income tax for a period of five consecutive years.

2. Business income tax: The maximum rate of income tax, including all forms of surtax, payable by a productive enterprise is not to exceed 18 percent of its total annual income, compared to 32.5 percent for ordinary profit-seeking enterprises.

3. Tax exemption for undistributed profit: The amount reinvested for productive purposes is deductible from taxable income.

4. Tax deduction of exports: Within certain limits a deduction from taxable income of 2 percent of annual export proceeds is permissible.

5. Exemption or reduction of stamp tax: This tax is either waived or reduced in a large number of cases.

6. Tax exemption of foreign currency debt: Productive enterprises are allowed to set aside 7 percent of their profits before taxation of the unpaid balance of foreign currency debt, calculated in local currency, as a reserve against possible loss caused by exchange rate revision.

The response of industry to export expansion in the early 1960s was still slow. In 1965, the statute was revised and its scope expanded. The Kaohsiung Export Processing Zone was set up within which no duties were imposed on imports. Development strategy at the time was entirely export-oriented.

Tax Reduction and Refunds

As a result of the statute for investment encouragement and the tax and duty refunds for exportation, a large proportion of the taxes were reduced, as shown in Table 4.1. Note that the highest income tax reductions occurred in 1963 and 1967, being 25.2 percent and 23.4 percent, respectively. In the 1970s, the income tax reduction was about 15 percent,

Table 4.1 Tax Reduction and Refunds
(as Percentage of the Corresponding Tax)

(percent)

Fiscal Year	Income Tax	Stamp Tax	Customs Duties	Commodity Tax	Total Refund in the Four Taxes
1955	–	–	2.3	0.2	1.5
1956	–	–	4.2	0.3	2.6
1957	–	–	2.9	3.0	2.9
1958	–	–	6.6	2.8	5.1
1960	–	–	13.5	8.5	11.5
1961	2.4	25.3	14.5	12.5	11.9
1962	21.5	37.6	20.3	24.3	23.2
1963	25.2	16.5	21.6	13.0	19.0
1964	17.3	20.3	38.8	18.0	26.4
1965	17.2	20.3	31.0	21.2	24.5
1966	21.4	51.1	32.6	20.1	28.1
1967	23.4	49.7	40.5	22.0	32.2
1968	19.0	48.2	39.2	23.0	31.1
1969	14.6	45.4	36.4	18.7	26.6
1970	15.1	52.2	49.2	25.1	34.1
1971	13.5	73.5	77.3	34.3	47.5
1972	14.9	60.0	86.1	37.3	52.4
1973	15.9	57.0	72.3	37.6	48.0
1974	22.0	50.9	46.2	31.7	36.9
1975	12.2	51.8	54.6	37.7	38.2
1976	15.3	48.7	42.2	37.3	34.3
1977	12.7	50.5	57.2	40.6	40.0
1978	14.9	34.2	40.5	36.0	31.8
1979	13.2	12.8	40.3	35.2	29.9

Note: Fiscal year 1958 runs July 1958-June 1959; fiscal year 1960 runs July 1959-
June 1960, due to the change in fiscal year system.
Source: Department of Statistics, Ministry of Finance, *Yearbook of Financial Sta-
tistics of the Republic of China, 1979* (1980).

although it jumped to 22 percent in 1974 as a result of higher earnings in the boom year of 1973.

Customs duties exempted and refunded increased rapidly from 1971 to 1973 because of the rapid expansion of exports relative to imports. Because of the decrease in the growth of exports in 1974, a sudden reduction of the percentage of total refund in the four taxes in 1974 took place in spite of increased total tariff revenue caused by the higher price of oil.

The refund on the commodity tax had the same tendency as that on customs duties. The refund of all four taxes in the boom period, 1971 to 1973, accounted for about 50 percent of the total revenue from all four taxes. However, after the peak year of 1972, the tax refund began to decrease. In 1979 the tax refund was reduced to only about 30 percent of the taxes.

The basic policy in recent years has been to reduce the tariff rate on necessary imports of raw materials and intermediate inputs, so as not to refund the tariff levied. Further measures have been taken along this line since 1976, and they will be intensified in the future.

Nominal Rate of Protection

When a tariff is levied on an imported commodity, the domestic price of that commodity will be raised higher than the international price. Therefore, for those internationally traded commodities, we can compare the ratio of domestic price to international price to see the degree of protection. In this sense, the ratio of domestic price to international price minus one is referred to as the rate of nominal protection; that is, a higher rate of nominal protection means a higher degree of protection. The nominal rates of protection for the manufacturing sector as a whole are shown in Table 4.2. Two sets of calculations are done, using domestic sales and exports as weights in the calculation.

The nominal rate of protection changed appreciably during the 1960s (1961 to 1971). The nominal rate of protection for manufacturing weighted by domestic sales dropped from

Table 4.2 Nominal Rate of Protection of Manufacturing
(Ratio of Domestic Prices to International Prices −1)

Item	1961	1966	1971
Nominal Rate of Protection Weighted by Domestic Sales			
Manufacturing (including food processing)	0.535	0.395	0.300
Manufacturing (excluding food processing)	0.384	0.309	0.285
Nominal Rate of Protection Weighted by Exports			
Manufacturing (including food processing)	0.563	0.391	0.360
Manufacturing (excluding food processing)	0.330	0.331	0.373

Source: See Shirley W.Y. Kuo, "Economic Growth and Structural Change in the Republic of China," Appendix II A (World Bank, 1979; mimeo.).

0.535 in 1961 to 0.395 in 1966 and further to 0.300 in 1971. The decrease during 1961 to 1966 was larger than from 1966 to 1971. The nominal rates of protection weighted by exports were similar and showed the same decreasing tendency. The high rate of protection in 1961 was due to the high rate of protection given to food processing at that time. If food processing is excluded, the rate of protection is reduced considerably.

Of four categories of manufacturing products — export competing, export-import competing, import competing, and nonimport competing[1] — it is interesting to observe that the highest rate of protection was for export competing industries, i.e., those industries for which the ratio of exports to domestic production was greater than 0.1. Import competing industries, whose imports to domestic use ratio was greater than 0.1, had the lowest rate of protection. Export-import competing industries, i.e., those that were both import competing and export competing, ranked second in

Table 4.3 Nominal Rate of Protection in Four Categories (Ratio of Domestic Prices to International Prices -1)

Item	1961	1966	1971
1. Export competing	0.574	0.386	0.293
2. Export-import competing	0.288	0.288	0.248
3. Import competing	0.266	0.178	0.178
4. Nonimport competing	0.149	0.106	0.205

Source: Same as Table 4.2.

protection. All other industries, classified as nonimport competing, ranked third (see Table 4.3).

The difference in rates among these four categories was much greater in 1961, but it decreased considerably in 1971. The rate for export competing industry was high in 1961 because of high rates for monosodium glutamate, sugar, nonalcoholic beverages, and miscellaneous fabrics. Monosodium glutamate and sugar kept high rates throughout the period, although their share in manufacturing decreased tremendously. The rates of protection for nonalcoholic beverages and miscellaneous fabrics decreased appreciably by 1971, thus causing the decrease of the average rate in this category.

Within the category of export-import competing, the rate of protection for artificial fabrics was the highest, particularly in 1961. Also high in 1961 were those for woolen fabrics and household electric appliances.

Special Export Loans

A special export loan program was initiated in 1957. Favorable interest rates for export financing have been available since then. However, the proportion of these loans has been relatively small, especially as compared with that in Korea. After 1974, outstanding loans under favorable

Table 4.4   Favorable Interest Rate Export Loans

End of Year	Favorable Interest Rate Export Loan (in millions of NT dollars)	Total Loan (in millions of NT dollars)	Percentage of Favorable Interest Rate Export Loan to Total Loan
1972	6,544	104,599	6.3
1973	8,742	151,514	5.8
1974	7,470	214,759	3.5
1975	8,000	284,507	2.8
1976	8,857	317,704	2.8
1977	11,108	375,892	3.0
1978	12,947	470,186	2.8
1979	12,398	544,650	2.3

Source: Economic Research Department, The Central Bank of China, *Financial Statistics Monthly, Taiwan District, The Republic of China*, various years.

rates in Taiwan were reduced to 3 percent or less of the total outstanding, as can be seen in Table 4.4.

Easier Availability of Funds to Private Enterprises

In the 1960s, as a result of the government policy to encourage private industry, the composition of loans given by all banks was modified to favor private enterprises. The percentage of loans going to private enterprises increased from 24 percent in 1953 to 77 percent in 1979 (see Table 4.5). Furthermore, the features of private enterprise liabilities also underwent a gradual transformation. Loans from banks increased from 32.3 percent in 1964 to 37.5 percent in 1969, while loans from households decreased from 36.7 percent to 22.5 percent. As the interest rate in unorganized markets like the household sector is much higher than that of bank loans (about twice as high), an increase in the proportion of bank loans and a decrease in the

Table 4.5 Loans to Private and Public Enterprises
by All Banks, 1953—1979

(percent)

End of Year	Bank Loans to Private Enterprises	Bank Loans to Public Enterprises
1953	24.2	75.8
1955	31.7	68.3
1960	47.0	53.0
1965	70.7	29.3
1970	77.6	22.4
1975	78.0	22.0
1979	77.0	23.0

Sources: Economic Planning Council, *Taiwan Statistical Data Book, 1977*, p. 141; Council for Economic Planning and Development, *Taiwan Statistical Data Book, 1980*, p. 145.

proportion of household loans means that loans are actually available at a lower interest rate. An increase in the share of foreign loans also contributed to an easing of financial availability.

The 1960s Foreign Exchange Policy

The policy change from import substitution to export promotion was also reflected in the 1960s foreign exchange policy, characterized by the adoption of a simple exchange rate and an avoidance of overvaluation of domestic currency. When the domestic currency is artificially overvalued, exporters receive less domestic currency than they should and importers pay less domestic currency than they should. Therefore, an overvaluation of domestic currency discourages exports and encourages imports.

The real effective exchange rate is a weighted average of various foreign currencies with the relation of foreign inflation rates to domestic rates being taken into account. When this rate exceeds 100, it means that the domestic currency is overvalued, so that exports are artificially discouraged. But when this rate is below 100, it means that domestic currency is undervalued, so that exports are artificially encouraged. Viewing the year 1970 as an equilibrium year (because Taiwan had a trade balance, i.e., imports equaled exports, in 1970), we show the real effective exchange rate of the period 1965–79 in Figure 4.1. We can see that during the second half of the 1960s the real effective exchange rates all remained around 100, the ideal level. That is, there was neither artificial encouragement nor artificial discouragement of exports through the foreign exchange rate. The abrupt surge of the real effective exchange rate in 1974 was due to a drastically higher domestic inflation rate in that year. The rate went down after 1975, and the domestic inflation rate was only about 3 percent on the average during 1975–78.

Fig. 4.1   Real Effective Exchange Rate of New Taiwan Dollar

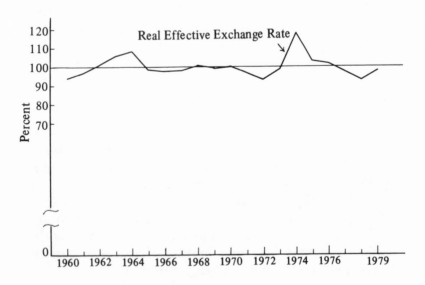

Note: Export values are used as weights.

In short, a multiple foreign exchange system was carefully and successfully transferred into a unified exchange system in 1961. Also during the 1960s, the foreign exchange rate was maintained at an acceptable level so that exports were not artificially discouraged through overvaluation of domestic currency.

In addition to the successful adoption of a unitary exchange rate, government policies of the 1960s included the encouragement of private industry by making funds more available to private enterprises and export promotion by reducing tariffs on necessary imports of raw materials and by reducing income taxes and certain customs duties and commodities taxes for productive businesses. Import-substitution policies were gradually replaced by export-promoting policies.

5

Growth and Income Distribution, 1964–79

The detailed household survey data available after 1964 make it possible to move beyond the descriptive treatment of the 1950s and early 1960s to a more analytical assessment of the relationship between growth and the family distribution of income for the 1964–79 period.

Linking Growth with Income Distribution

Among the wide variety of distribution factors in economics, functional distribution and family income distribution are the two major ones. Functional distribution is the study of the division of income between income from labor (wages) and income from property, which is largely determined by the type and speed of economic growth. Family income distribution is the study of the division of income by dividing the income of families into size categories. It is the basis for the analysis of income distribution.

Academic interest has centered for a long time on functional distribution. Only recently has family income distribution received much academic and government concern. Elsewhere we have attempted to link functional distribution with family income distribution, thus linking growth with income distribution.[1] The essence of our thesis will be briefly explained below.

The total income of a family can be broken down into wage income and property income. Comparing only wage incomes of all families, we can obtain a distribution of wage income, while, likewise, comparing only property incomes of all families can give a distribution of property income. The Gini coefficient is used as the indicator of income equality: The greater the coefficient, the less even the income distribution. As is shown in Figure 5.1, the Gini coefficient is the ratio of the area enclosed by the diagonal line and the Lorenz curve to the area of the triangle, namely the shaded area ABC to the area of triangle ABD. Using the Gini coefficient as the indicator of income inequality, we can

Fig. 5.1   Gini Coefficient and Lorenz Curve

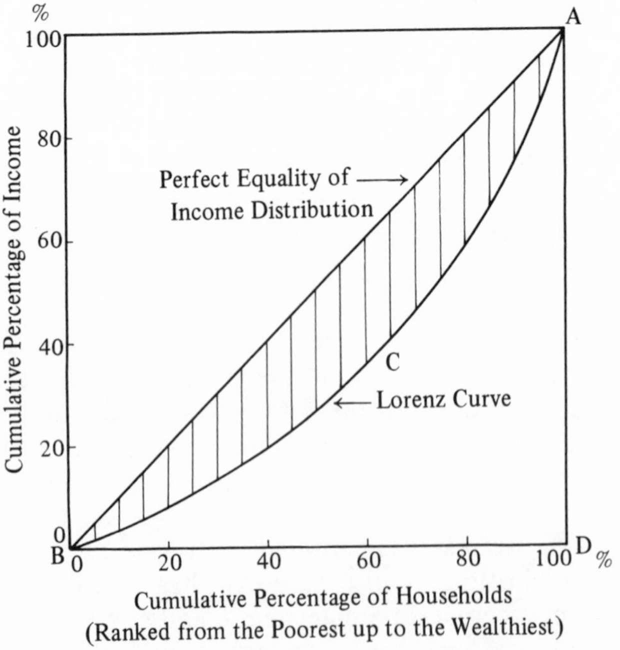

Cumulative Percentage of Households
(Ranked from the Poorest up to the Wealthiest)

Diagrammatically, a Lorenz curve is derived by plotting the cumulative percentage of the households (ranked from the poorest up to the wealthiest), shown on the horizontal axis, against the cumulative percentage share of the total income they receive, shown on the vertical axis. The diagonal line represents the perfect equality of income distribution, where Gini coefficient equals zero.

calculate wage Gini and property Gini to show the degree of inequality of wage income distribution and property income distribution, respectively. The link between growth and distribution is made by the following decomposition equation:

$$G_y = \phi_W G_W + \phi_\pi G_\pi \qquad (5.1)$$
$$(\phi_W + \phi_\pi = 1)$$

where

G_y = Gini coefficient of the whole economy
G_W = Gini coefficient of the wage income distribution
G_π = Gini coefficient of the property income distribution
ϕ_W = share of wage income in the total income
ϕ_π = share of property income in the total income

The inequality in wage income is smaller than the inequality in property income (G_W is less than G_π), so that an increase in the share of wage income will reduce the inequality of family income distribution. The reason that inequality in wage income is less than that of property income is that wage income inequality depends on differences in the wage earner's age, sex, level of education, skills, and so on, while property income inequality depends on differences in the ownership of properties (land and capital). Inequality arising from the former factors is less than the inequality arising from the latter.

Therefore, what we examine in this chapter is how much smaller the wage Gini was than the property Gini and in what way the wage share changed. What equation 5.1 means is that the degree of inequality of family income is determined by the degree of inequality of wage and property income and also by the relative share of wage income in family income. In essence, the equation states that the inequality of total family income is the sum of the inequalities of both wage and property incomes.

This equation attributes the changes in the family distribution of income over time to two distinct types of effects that are relevant to growth. First, an increase in the share of wage income will be favorable to family income distribution; and the larger the difference of $G_\pi - G_W$, the larger that effect will be. This change in family income distribution of the whole economy caused by the change in the share of wage income is referred to as the "functional distribution effect." Second, a change in the distribution of wage income or distribution of property income will affect the family income distribution of the whole economy. This effect will be referred to as the "factor Gini effect."[2] The change in family income distribution may thus be traced in part to changes in the functional distribution of income and in part to changes in the patterns of family ownership of labor, capital, land, and so on.

When wage income is distributed more equally than property income, a change in the functional distribution favoring labor, indicated by a rise in the distributive share of wage income to total income, will always serve to improve income distribution. In fact, this relation establishes the necessary condition for the notion—usually accepted uncritically—that any change favoring labor's share in income necessarily improves income distribution.

One source of real-world complexity must be accommodated when the aforementioned relations are applied to a dualistic LDC, such as Taiwan, the Republic of China. This complexity can be traced to the dualistic locational aspect of families and production activities and to the importance of agricultural income. Urban families receive income primarily from nonagricultural production, that is, from wage and property income from urban industry and services. Rural families usually receive income from both agricultural and nonagricultural sources, that is, merged wage and property income from agriculture and wage and property income from rural industry and services. This additional complexity in the real world is the motivation for treating the whole economy as being composed of three models: urban households, rural households, and all households. The decomposition can be directly applied to urban households. But because the models of all households and rural households also have the additional and important source of agricultural income, the analysis of these two groups must be modified. It is substantially enriched in the process.

For nonagricultural production the functional distributive shares of wage and property income will be explicitly treated as above; income from agriculture will not, however, be functionally distinguished. This treatment is based on two considerations, the first practical, the second theoretical. First, in the farm-family type of agricultural activity, property and wage income can be disentangled only by using highly artificial procedures of imputation. Second, the essence of development in the dualistic economy is the gradual reallocation of resources, particularly labor, from agricultural to nonagricultural activities. A declining distributive share of agricultural income in total income $[\Phi_a]$ is a proxy for this reallocation.

Changes in the inequality of total income may thus be traced to three sources. The first is the continuous reallocation of labor from agricultural to nonagricultural activities, proxied by the decline in the share of agricultural income in total income as the economic center of gravity shifts from agriculture to nonagriculture. The second is the changing impact of the functional distribution of income, traced to such factors as capital accumulation, technological change, and population growth. The third is the impact of changes in the distribution of income among factors of production—capital and labor—as traced to abrupt changes in asset structure arising from different patterns of private and public saving for the formation of physical and human capital. For the first two forces, the link of growth theory to income distribution is quite direct. For the third force, the relation of traditional economic analysis to income distribution is more indirect and complicated.

**Improved Distribution Seen
in Wage and Property Incomes**

Sample survey data on household income in Taiwan—

collected by the Directorate-General of Budget, Accounting, and Statistics (DGBAS) for 1964, 1966, 1968, 1970, 1972, 1974, 1976, and 1978 — have been processed in accordance with the analytical framework presented in the preceding section.[3] The following assumptions were made in transforming the raw data into a simplifying three-model framework. First, a category of unallocable miscellaneous income was ignored, as was the agricultural income of urban families. Both were quantitatively small. Second, no account was taken of intersectoral payments, such as the inclusion in rural wage income of the urban income of farmers' daughters. Isolating such payments in the data was impossible. Third, as pointed out before, agricultural income was not functionally disaggregated into wage and property shares. For farm-family agriculture, such a separation would have entailed a rather arbitrary imputation procedure.

Table 5.1 shows the necessary information for the application of equation 5.1 to the Taiwan economy. It shows the magnitude of Gini coefficients and the shares of wage income, property income, and agricultural income over time. Families are classified into all households (for the whole economy), urban households, and rural households. Figures 5.2 and 5.3 provide a graphic depiction of these time series. The results show the following facts:

1. For each and every kind of household, the wage Gini has been considerably smaller than the property Gini for the past fifteen years (see Figure 5.2). This means that wage income was more equally distributed than property income in Taiwan.

2. For each and every kind of household, the share of wage income had a tendency to increase during the past fifteen years (see Figure 5.3). The share of wage income in rural households increased significantly after 1968, taking the place of the originally large agricultural income share.

When a longer period is observed, we know that the share of wage income in the national income increased from 40.8

percent in 1951 to 60.8 percent in 1979. The share of property income dropped accordingly. That is, the share of wage income increased at an annual rate of 1.4 percent, while the share of property income decreased at an annual rate of 1.5 percent. As wage income is more equally distributed than property income and the share of the former increased over time, we know that the increasing share of wage income was a basic cause of the improved income distribution in Taiwan.

It is self-evident that governments of most LDCs, despite their limited fiscal capacity, can directly affect the distribution of income through taxes and transfers. But the main inference to be drawn from the findings here is that a change in the growth path is likely to be the most effective method of tackling the maldistribution of income. The experience of Taiwan, the Republic of China—unusually low Gini coefficients and no significant transfers through welfare payments—bears out our conviction that significant and sustained changes in income distribution equity are achievable mainly through the modification of the basic forces underlying the pattern of growth, at least in non-socialist mixed economies.

Improved Distribution Associated with Industrialization and Urbanization

The causes of the inequality of family income were explicitly traced in the previous section to wage- and property-income components. In this section, a more aggregate view is taken by de-emphasizing these factor components and concentrating on the sectoral decomposition. This aggregate view facilitates tracing the inequality of family income to various homogeneous categories of income recipients, such as farm and nonfarm families.

The income gaps between families in different sectors and locations are an important and dynamic economic force that causes the urbanization of the population and the shift of farm workers to nonfarm activities. If labor were completely mobile, the income gaps would tend to be small. But

Table 5.1   Gini Coefficients and the Shares of Wage, Property
and Agricultural Incomes, 1964—1978

Item	1964	1966	1968	1970
All Households				
Total Gini	0.3208	0.3226	0.3260	0.2928
Wage Gini	0.2365	0.2697	0.2932	0.2775
Property Gini	0.4487	0.4104	0.4598	0.4278
Agricultural Gini	0.3543	0.3410	0.1817	0.0655
Wage share[a]	0.4324	0.4760	0.5066	0.5454
Property share	0.2401	0.2557	0.2777	0.2558
Agricultural share	0.2754	0.2118	0.1523	0.1307
Urban Households				
Total Gini	0.3288	0.3236	0.3296	0.2794
Wage Gini	n.a.	0.2797	0.2732	0.2328
Property Gini	n.a.	0.4193	0.4246	0.3689
Wage share[a]	0.5729	0.5925	0.5673	0.6016
Property share	0.3225	0.3218	0.3366	0.3022
Rural Households				
Total Gini	0.3080	0.3200	0.2842	0.2772
Wage Gini	n.a.	0.1933	0.1880	0.2042
Property Gini	n.a.	0.3344	0.2775	0.3607
Agricultural Gini	n.a.	0.3534	0.3372	0.3138
Wage share[a]	0.2134	0.2016	0.3227	0.3602
Property share	0.1115	0.1000	0.0994	0.1029
Agricultural share	0.6468	0.6595	0.5263	0.4869

n.a. Not available.

a. The relative shares do not quite add up to 1 because the merged category of mixed incomes, which constitute less than 10 percent of the total, was neglected. In addition, the share of agricultural income in the total income of nonfarm households is uniformly small, which conforms to the assumption about the income of urban households.

1972	1974	1976	1978[b]	Item
				All Households
0.2897	0.2996	0.2894	0.2887	Total Gini
0.2604	0.2695	0.2675	0.2789	Wage Gini
0.4235	0.4284	0.4072	0.3777	Property Gini
0.1105	0.1596	0.0965	0.0718	Agricultural Gini
0.5895	0.6031	0.5948	0.6210	Wage share[a]
0.2577	0.2477	0.2535	0.2551	Property share
0.1027	0.1018	0.0885	0.0729	Agricultural share
				Urban Households
0.2813	0.2967	0.2804	0.2802	Total Gini
0.2349	0.2534	0.2396	0.2547	Wage Gini
0.3874	0.4044	0.3729	0.3384	Property Gini
0.6335	0.6557	0.6404	0.6533	Wage share[a]
0.2975	0.2810	0.2865	0.2847	Property share
				Rural Households
0.2844	0.2887	0.2851	0.2851	Total Gini
0.2378	0.1927	0.2235	0.2714	Wage Gini
0.3477	0.3578	0.3343	0.3712	Property Gini
0.2983	0.3482	0.3311	0.2874	Agricultural Gini
0.4226	0.3728	0.4042	0.4776	Wage share[a]
0.1072	0.1019	0.1157	0.1239	Property share
0.4230	0.4810	0.4136	0.3342	Agricultural share

b. Excluding Taipei City.
Sources: Department of Budget, Accounting and Statistics, Taiwan Provincial Government, *Report on the Survey of Family Income and Expenditure, Taiwan Province, Republic of China;* Bureau of Budget, Accounting and Statistics, Taipei City Government, *Report on the Survey of Family Income and Expenditure and Personal Income Distribution of Taipei City,* various years.

Fig. 5.2 Gini Coefficients of Wage Income, Property Income, and Agricultural Income

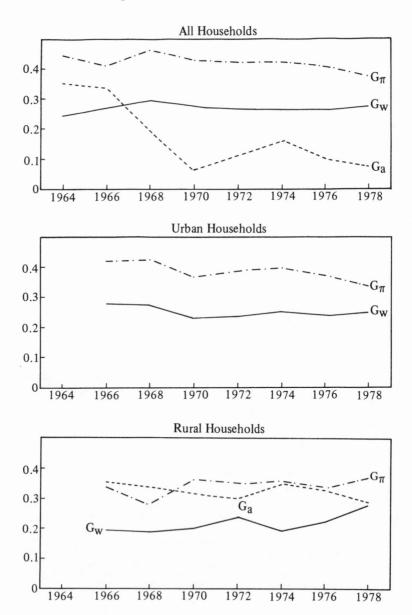

All Households

Urban Households

Rural Households

Fig. 5.3 The Shares of Wage Income, Property Income, and Agricultural Income

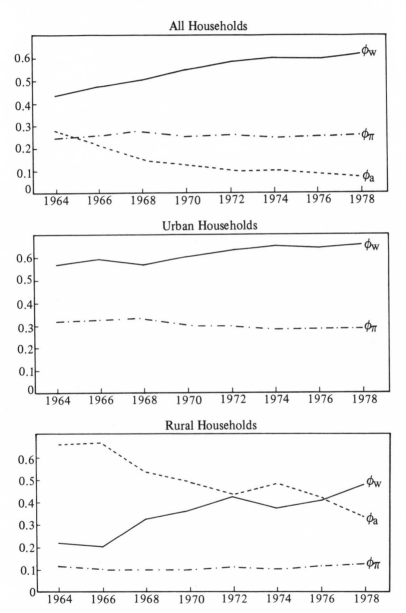

All Households

Urban Households

Rural Households

the mobility of labor is often impeded by such factors as traditional ideologies and social systems, particularly during the early stages of economic development. Consequently it is never perfect. Because it is imperfect, part of the labor force remains in the lower-productivity sectors and causes the gaps in income between sectors to widen.

In Taiwan, the income gap between farm and nonfarm families widened during 1964–79 because farm income was growing at a slower rate than nonfarm income. The income gap between rural and urban sectors also widened. But despite these widening gaps between sectors, the inequality of income significantly declined at the national level. How could this have happened? How could the inequality of income decline for the entire country as the inequality of income increased between farm and nonfarm families? This section probes the reasons for that reduction in the inequality of family income by using a sectoral decomposition formula that measures two main effects: the inequality among sectors and that within sectors. The root causes of the inequality of family income will thus be explained by analyzing an intersectoral effect and an intrasectoral effect.

The intersectoral effect, consisting of a family-weight effect and an income-disparity effect, is caused by changes in the shares of different sectors in the total number of families and in total family income. The family-weight effect is caused by changes in the weights of sectors as measured by the percentages of families in each sector. When an economy develops and labor is reallocated, the modern sectors expand while the more traditional sectors shrink. This shift of family weights among sectors has an effect on the distribution of income. In contrast, the income-disparity effect is caused by changes in the income parities among sectors. The gap of average family income between two sectors arises principally from productivity differences. Because of the differences in the technology used in agricultural and nonagricultural production, labor productivity usually is higher and growing more rapidly in the modern sector than in the traditional sector. That, too, has an effect on the distribution of income.

The intrasectoral effect is caused by changes in the inequality of income within each sector and can be explained by numerous causative elements. Its principal cause, however, is the heterogeneity of families arising from differences in the ownership of assets and in the ownership of labor embodying particular characteristics.

This section is devoted principally to a study of the proximate cause of the reduction in the inequality of income in Taiwan. An attempt is made to decompose national income according to classifications of income recipients by sector. The sectoral classifications are based on farm and nonfarm activity and on the degree of urbanization—measured by rural, semiurban, and urban residence. Changes in the inequality of income over time will be analyzed in relation to industrialization and urbanization.

The sectoral decomposition method of Fei, Ranis, and Kuo[4] is applied to decompose the economy into farm and nonfarm sectors and then urban, semiurban, and rural sectors. The degree of income inequality of each sector and the income share of farm and nonfarm sectors are shown in Table 5.2. A comparison of farm and nonfarm sectors can be summarized as follows:

1. The income was more equally distributed in the farm sector than in the nonfarm sector before 1971; however, income distribution in the farm sector tended to be more unequal afterward except in 1974, the year of highest inflation.
2. The percentage of farm families in the total declined. This is a typical and significant characteristic of industrialization.
3. The per family income of the nonfarm sector was always higher than that of the farm sector.
4. The income distributions of both the farm and nonfarm sectors improved, but the speed of improvement was less for the farm sector than for the nonfarm sector.

Because of the importance of industrialization and ur-

Table 5.2   Gini Coefficients and Family Shares
by Sector, 1964—1978

Year	Gini Coefficient of the Whole Economy	Gini Coefficient of Farm Sector	Gini Coefficient of Nonfarm Sector	Family Share of Farm Families in Total	Family Share of Nonfarm Families in Total
1964	0.3208	0.3080	0.3288	0.3959	0.6041
1966	0.3226	0.3200	0.3236	0.3093	0.6907
1968	0.3260	0.2842	0.3296	0.3154	0.6846
1970	0.2928	0.2772	0.2794	0.3091	0.6909
1972	0.2897	0.2844	0.2813	0.2588	0.7412
1974	0.2996	0.2887	0.2967	0.2280	0.7720
1976	0.2894	0.2851	0.2804	0.2446	0.7554
1978	0.2887[a]	0.2851[a]	0.2802[a]	0.2006	0.7994

a   Taipei City is not included.
Source: Same as Table 5.1.

banization in economic growth, the effect of urbanization on the distribution of income should be explored. To identify the relations between urbanization and income distribution, the income data based on city-town-village classifications were compiled from the original questionnaires of the DGBAS survey for 1966 and 1972. Table 5.3 gives the results, which may be summarized as follows:

1. The inequality of the distribution of income within the more urban sectors was not necessarily worse than that within the less urban sectors.
2. The total share of families in the most urban sector increased, and the share of families in the rural sector declined over time—a natural tendency of urbanization.

Table 5.3 Decomposition Analysis, by Degree of Urbanization in the Three-Sector Classification, 1966 and 1972

Variable and Sector	Notation	1966	1972
Total Gini	G	0.3237	0.3018
Sectoral Gini			
Urban sector	G_1	0.3134	0.2974
Semiurban sector	G_2	0.3182	0.2719
Rural sector	G_3	0.3316	0.2800
Total coefficient	I	0.6610	0.6290
Sectoral coefficient			
Urban sector	I_1	0.6505	0.6182
Semiurban sector	I_2	0.6432	0.5433
Rural sector	I_3	0.6684	0.5628
Sectoral family fraction	h		
Urban sector	h_1	0.2826	0.3798
Semiurban sector	h_2	0.4137	0.3434
Rural sector	h_3	0.3037	0.2768

Source: Calculated from the original questionnaires of the DGBAS surveys.

3. The per family incomes of the more urban sectors generally were higher than those of the less urban sectors.
4. Income inequality within sectors improved for every sector over time.

Causes Traced to the Farm-Nonfarm Decomposition

During the 1964–79 period, as we have already seen, overall income inequality declined significantly. But with farm-family income growing less rapidly than nonfarm-family income, the income gap between the two kinds of families widened. In addition, the income gaps among family groups in different locations, classified by the degree of urbanization, widened during the same period. The widening gap caused by industrialization and urbanization can be observed through changes in income disparities, an indicator suggested by Kuznets, in sectors classified by farm and nonfarm families and by different degrees of urbanization.[5]

Disparities in the incomes of farm and nonfarm families increased from 1964 to 1979, indicating increasing inequality between the two sectors. Income disparities by degree of urbanization show that the widening was most prevalent between the most urban and the most rural sectors. Levels and trends in income differences among the sectors reveal that per family income was rising at a higher-than-average rate in both the nonfarm sector and the most urban sector. In contrast, per family income was rising at a lower-than-average rate in the farm sector and the most rural sector.

A question is often raised, then, as to how overall income inequality can be reduced in a dynamic economy in which structural change has been occurring at a rapid pace. In order to identify the basic causes, the sectoral decomposition method of Fei, Ranis, and Kuo is applied to analyze the causes of income inequality reduction for the period 1964-79. The results obtained show the following facts:

1. One favorable factor contributing to the reduction in income inequality was the reduction in internal inequality within both the farm and nonfarm sectors. The contribution of each sector to the total intrasectoral inequality reduction was 9 percent and 91 percent respectively.

2. The change in the weights of farm and nonfarm family numbers and the widening of the income gap between the two sectors adversely affected the distribution of income. However, the rate of adverse effect was not very large, accounting for only 20 percent of the total change.

3. The essential cause of the reduction in income inequality in the Republic of China was the reduction in income inequality within the nonfarm sector. Given

this finding, we shall further explore the changes in nonagricultural income.

A characteristic of Taiwan's farm-family income is that it contains quite a large portion of nonagricultural income. The portion of nonagricultural income in farm-family income was 34.1 percent in 1966 and increased to 72.7 percent in 1979.[6] Table 5.4 shows the detail of its composition by different farm income levels. The lower income level predominated in 1966 and up until 1975. However, nonagricultural income became an important source of farm-family income afterwards. Table 5.4 also shows that almost 99 percent of nonfarm income is from nonagricultural activities; thus, agricultural income in nonfarm income is negligible.

During the period 1966–79, per family income of both farm and nonfarm sectors showed a considerable increase in all income brackets. However, nonagricultural income was the major source of increased farm-family income. The nonagricultural share of farm-family income grew 988 percent; agricultural income alone grew only 111 percent (at current prices) over this period. Thus, the 409 percent growth rate of farm-family income was completely attributable to the growth of nonagricultural income of farm families.

The higher growth rates of incomes from nonagricultural activities in the lower-income family groups indicate that a relatively rapid rate of initial employment generation for members of the lower-income groups and the subsequent changes in their wages in the later period helped create a high overall growth rate. During the period under observation, rapid labor absorption first eliminated unemployment; newcomers and formerly unemployed individuals were absorbed mainly by the nonagricultural sector, particularly by light manufacturing industries.

As the economy grew, unskilled labor ultimately became relatively scarcer as the wage rate of unskilled labor rose. Undoubtedly, the rapid absorption of unskilled labor at low opportunity costs contributed substantially to the rise in

Table 5.4   Sources of Farm and Nonfarm Incomes

(percent)

Ten Equal Divisions of Family Numbers	1966			
	Farm Family		Nonfarm Family	
	% of Agricultural Income to Total Farm Family Income	% of Non-agricultural Income to Total Farm Family Income	% of Agricultural Income to Total Nonfarm Family Income	% of Non-agricultural Income to Total Nonfarm Family Income
The top 10% of families	67.6	32.4	1.8	98.2
The 2nd 10% of families	70.2	29.8	2.3	97.7
The 3rd 10% of families	70.1	29.9	2.2	97.8
The 4th 10% of families	68.5	31.5	1.7	98.3
The 5th 10% of families	65.5	34.5	2.4	97.6
The 6th 10% of families	64.3	35.7	1.8	98.2
The 7th 10% of families	61.0	39.0	2.4	97.6
The 8th 10% of families	57.3	42.7	3.0	97.0
The 9th 10% of families	55.3	44.7	2.8	97.2
The lowest 10% of families	54.7	45.3	2.9	97.1
Total	65.9	34.1	2.2	97.8

Source: Department of Budget, Accounting and Statistics, Taiwan Provincial Government, *Report on the Survey of Family Income and Expenditure, Taiwan Province, Republic of China* (1966 and 1979).

1979				
Farm Family		Nonfarm Family		
% of Agricultural Income to Total Farm Family Income	% of Non-agricultural Income to Total Farm Family Income	% of Agricultural Income to Total Nonfarm Family Income	% of Non-agricultural Income to Total Nonfarm Family Income	Ten Equal Divisions of Family Numbers
24.4	75.6	0.8	99.2	The top 10% of families
27.9	72.1	1.0	99.0	The 2nd 10% of families
26.8	73.2	1.5	98.5	The 3rd 10% of families
25.5	74.5	1.5	98.5	The 4th 10% of families
27.5	72.5	1.3	98.7	The 5th 10% of families
25.8	74.2	1.7	98.3	The 6th 10% of families
28.9	71.1	1.7	98.3	The 7th 10% of families
32.9	67.1	2.2	97.8	The 8th 10% of families
31.4	68.6	2.7	97.3	The 9th 10% of families
33.7	66.3	2.4	97.6	The lowest 10% of families
27.3	72.7	1.4	98.6	Total

relative incomes of the lower-income families in both the farm and nonfarm sectors. At the same time, the strategy of decentralization of economic development was one of the essential factors contributing to the reduction of income inequality.

Labor Absorption and Female Participation

The changes in the agricultural and manufacturing labor structure give a view of the kind of labor being absorbed. As can be seen in Table 5.5, from 1966 to 1980 the agricultural labor force gained a much higher percentage of older persons. The largest outmigration from the agricultural sector was observed in the group of females under 24 years of age.

On the other hand, as shown in Table 5.6, in manufacturing industry during the same period, the proportion of those 30 years old and older decreased from 47.3 percent in 1966 to 36.7 percent in 1972 and then increased to 38.2 percent in

Table 5.5 Agricultural Labor Classified by Age and by Sex

(percent)

	Year	Total Agricultural Labor	Age		
			15-24	25-29	Over 30
Total	1966	100.0	26.1	14.1	59.8
	1972	100.0	22.5	8.6	68.9
	1980	100.0	12.2	11.2	76.6
Male	1966	100.0	20.7	14.9	64.4
	1972	100.0	18.4	8.9	72.7
	1980	100.0	11.5	11.7	76.8
Female	1966	100.0	39.7	12.1	48.2
	1972	100.0	30.2	8.1	61.7
	1980	100.0	14.2	10.2	75.6

Sources: Taiwan Provincial Labor Force Survey and Research Institute, *Quarterly Report on the Labor Force Survey in Taiwan, Republic of China* (October 1966 and October 1972); Directorate-General of Budget, Accounting and Statistics, Executive Yuan, *Monthly Bulletin of Labor Statistics, Republic of China* (November 1980).

1980. Meanwhile, the group of persons 15–24 years of age increased from 38.5 percent to 51.6 percent, but decreased to 43.2 percent in 1980. Manufacturing originally had a large proportion of young females. The rapid absorption of young females grew during the 1960s. In 1972, female workers under 24 years of age accounted for 74.2 percent of all female workers, although the situation had changed by 1980.

As Table 5.7 shows, the absorption of laborers under 24 years of age accounted for 66.3 percent of total labor absorption in the manufacturing industry during 1966–72; however, it declined to only 31.8 percent of labor absorbed during 1972–80. The percentage of young female absorption was higher, registering 79.0 percent of total female labor absorption in the period 1966–72.

The need for young female workers in manufacturing was well supported by the increasing supply of those workers in the labor market. This increase came from two sources. One is the higher participation rate; the other, the expansion of the female population aged 15 and over, particularly

Table 5.6 Manufacturing Labor Classified by Age and by Sex

(percent)

	Year	Total Manufacturing Labor	Age		
			15-24	25-29	Over 30
Total	1966	100.0	38.5	14.2	47.3
	1972	100.0	51.6	11.7	36.7
	1980	100.0	43.2	18.6	38.2
Male	1966	100.0	29.0	15.9	55.1
	1972	100.0	38.2	15.6	46.2
	1980	100.0	29.3	22.8	47.9
Female	1966	100.0	65.9	9.4	24.7
	1972	100.0	74.2	5.2	20.6
	1980	100.0	63.8	12.4	23.8

Source: Same as Table 5.5.

Table 5.7   Relative Weight of Labor Absorption in the
            Manufacturing Sector Classified by Age and
            by Sex

| Period | Increment of Employment (thousands) | | | |
| | Δ L | Δ Lj | | |
	Total	15-24	25-29	Over 30
1966-72				
Total	588	390	52	146
Male	293	157	44	92
Female	295	233	8	54
1972-80				
Total	930	296	259	375
Male	523	85	175	263
Female	407	211	84	112

Source: Same as Table 5.5.

the age group of 15–24 years. It can be shown that population growth accounted for 55 percent of the increase of the supply, and the remaining 45 percent can be accounted for by an increase in the participation rate.[7] The participation rates of females between the ages of 15 and 19 increased from 48.5 percent in 1966 to 53.7 percent in 1972, and those of females aged 20–24 increased from 41.3 percent in 1966 to 50.0 percent in 1972.

With respect to educational levels, females in the junior vocational school group had the most rapid rates of growth of participation in the labor force. Participation stood at 22.4 percent in 1964 and 54.2 percent in 1973, showing an increase of 240 percent. The junior high school group came next; the participation rate of this group rose from 23.2 percent to 43.8 percent. As can be seen from Table 5.8, the overall improvement in participation rates was realized

Relative Weight (percent)				Period
Δ Lj / Δ L				
Total	15-24	25-29	Over 30	
				1966-72
100.0	66.3	8.9	24.8	Total
100.0	53.6	15.0	31.4	Male
100.0	79.0	2.7	18.3	Female
				1972-80
100.0	31.8	27.9	40.3	Total
100.0	16.3	33.5	50.2	Male
100.0	51.9	20.6	27.5	Female

mostly by the increase in employment at the lower educational levels. The only reduction in participation rates was found among the senior high school group up until 1974. This was partly due to the sharp increase in the number of female graduates who decided to pursue higher education and partly due to the absence of vocational training in school. However, after 1974, the participation rate of the senior high school group increased. A higher female participation rate was observed in the category of junior college, university, and graduate school graduates. The rate has been rising in recent years, reaching 55.3 percent in 1980. The advancing educational level of females in the labor force is not only a notable sociological factor, but also an important factor for improving female income and thus reducing income inequality.

Changes in the composition of the labor force were only

Table 5.8   Female Labor Force Participation Rate by Education

(percent)

Educational Level	1964	1968	1972	1973	1974	1980
Illiterate	27.3	23.8	26.0	30.1	28.8	19.1
Self-educated	32.0	34.3	37.7	45.2	50.5	36.9
Primary school	41.3	43.5	45.1	49.4	47.0	36.8
Junior high school	23.2	41.3	39.5	42.9	43.8	50.8
Junior vocational school	22.4	43.8	49.6	54.2	51.4	
Senior high school	32.1	26.4	26.3	28.3	27.3	31.8
Senior vocational school	41.3	37.7	42.7	48.0	48.4	50.3
Normal school	60.9	66.7	68.2	67.0	62.9	
Junior college, university, and graduate school	38.0	33.5	40.9	44.8	43.4	55.3

Sources: Taiwan Provincial Labor Force Survey & Research Institute, *Quarterly Report on the Labor Force Survey in Taiwan,* various years; Directorate-General of Budget, Accounting and Statistics, Executive Yuan, *Monthly Bulletin of Labor Statistics, Republic of China* (November 1980).

part of the transformation of the Taiwanese economy in the course of economic development. The share of wages in national income increased over time, and the wage paid to unskilled labor rose as unskilled labor became increasingly scarce. The effects of structural change on income distribution can be analyzed by decomposing national income by recipient group and type of income. Using this decomposition we find that the major contribution to reduced income inequality was a reduction of inequality within each recipient group, especially within the nonfarm sector.

6
The Effects of Trade
on Economic Growth
and Labor Income

We have seen in the previous chapters that rapid labor absorption and increase in the share of wages in national income were essential causes for more equal income distribution amid rapid growth. It must be emphasized, however, that labor can be absorbed only when there is opportunity for work.

The traditional theory of production sees output as determined by the available quantities of production factors and the level of technology; that is, production factors determine output, but not the other way around. The theory is based on Say's Law, which states that supply creates its own demand. Thus, according to traditional theory, the amount of output produced is determined simply by factor availability and technology, and the amount of output that is technically producible is identically equal to the amount of output that will be produced. However, since the publication of Keynes's *General Theory of Employment, Interest and Money* (1935) and the Great Depression of the 1930s, we have become fully aware that Say's Law does not always hold true and that the production function alone cannot determine the amount of output realized; the size of demand is a decisive factor as well.

As demand is one of the two determinants of production, we should take a closer look at sources of demand. Sources of growth will be divided into four components: (1) domestic demand expansion, (2) export expansion, (3) import substitution, and (4) changes in technology.

Effects of Exports on Growth: An Aggregate Analysis

What are the sources of growth that have propelled Taiwan's industrialization? How much have exports contributed to its rapid growth and improved income distribution? In order to deal with these questions, this section will analyze the sources of growth of gross output for the period 1956-76.

The calculations are based on the absolute amount of change in a period in order to measure the absolute contributions of each source to the output expansion in that particular period. In addition, a "total method" is used to take care of all the direct and indirect contributions by each source and by each sector. Sources of growth are calculated for each of the fifty-eight production sectors in the economy for each period. The sum of the results of the fifty-eight sectors by each source provides the aggregate by each source for the total economy. These are shown in Table 6.1.

It is impressive to note that export expansion as a source of output expansion has become increasingly important. In

Table 6.1   Sources of Growth of Output Expansion

(percent)

Period	Output Expansion Due to Domestic Expansion	Output Expansion Due to Export Expansion	Output Expansion Due to Import Substitution	Output Expansion Due to Technological Change
1956-61	61.6	22.5	7.7	8.2
1961-66	63.2	35.0	0.5	1.3
1966-71	51.4	45.9	5.7	− 3.0
1971-76	34.7	67.7	− 2.4	0

Source: Calculated based on the Input-Output data consistently deflated into 1971 constant domestic prices.

the early period, 1956–61, the contribution of export expansion to output growth was 22.5 percent. It increased rapidly to 35.0 percent in 1961–66, 45.9 percent in 1966–71, and 67.7 percent in 1971–76. It is evident that after the 1960s, export expansion was a decisive factor in rapid growth, and in the 1970s its importance outweighed even domestic expansion. Import substitution was a trivial factor, although it did register a slight contribution in the 1950s.

Effects of Exports on Manufacturing Growth

It may be of interest to examine closely the sources of growth of manufacturing, as it has been the leading sector. In order for us to examine their characteristics, the subsectors of manufacturing have been classified in three different ways in this section. The classifying variables and corresponding categories are the following:

1. trade pattern: export competing, export-import competing, import competing, and nonimport competing;
2. degree of labor absorption: labor-absorbing industries and other industries; and
3. industry group: food processing, textiles, steel and iron, electrical machinery, machinery, intermediate goods, and final goods.

Decomposition by Trade Pattern

It is interesting to observe the following results from Table 6.2:

1. The contribution of export expansion was greatest in the export competing category throughout the whole period 1956–76. Export expansion in the export-import competing and import competing categories was also very high. This result indicates that there was a close relationship between exports and imports in Taiwan; that is, processing is an important element in the structure of Taiwan's economy.
2. The contribution of export expansion has been in-

Table 6.2 Sources of Manufacturing Output Growth
(by Trade Pattern)

(percent)

Period and Item	Domestic Demand Expansion	Export Expan- sion	Import Substitu- tion	Change in I-O Coefficients
1956-61				
Export competing	50.4	43.0	2.5	4.1
Export-import competing	46.2	24.3	23.4	6.1
Import competing	43.9	23.2	29.2	3.7
Nonimport competing	92.5	3.4	1.1	3.0
Manufacturing total	44.3	36.3	13.2	6.2
1961-71				
Export competing	35.6	67.1	1.6	− 4.3
Export-import competing	38.4	53.1	4.8	3.7
Import competing	37.3	36.0	17.7	9.0
Nonimport competing	91.0	13.9	1.4	− 6.3
Manufacturing total	36.9	51.5	7.6	4.0
1971-76				
Export competing	11.2	91.0	− 2.2	−
Export-import competing	23.9	76.3	− 0.2	−
Import competing	10.3	81.4	8.3	−
Nonimport competing	82.1	19.6	− 1.7	−
Manufacturing total	19.8	80.6	− 0.4	−

Notes:
1. Calculated from the 1971 constant domestic price I-O data for 1956, 1961, 1966, 1971 & 1976. All estimates of total contributions are arithmetic averages of the estimates derived by Laspeyres and Paasche versions. The estimates for 1961-71 are obtained by the chain measures of decompositions for the two periods.
2. The classifications of the four categories are based on 1971 ratios.
Source: See Table 6.1.

creasing rapidly over time for each and every category, showing an increasingly high dependence on exports.

3. A significant contribution of import substitution was observed for the import competing and export-import competing categories in the first period. Although the effect of import substitution on import competing industries decreased, it was always positive.

Decomposition by Degree of Labor Absorption

Thirty-seven industries were ranked as subsectors of labor-absorbing manufacturing. Labor-absorbing manufacturing industries are those that ranked in the first 10 percent of the thirty-seven industries in the absorption of labor, either in amount (1971) or in growth rate (1966–71).

The contribution of export expansion to the labor-absorbing manufacturing industries followed different patterns before and after 1961 (see Table 6.3). Prior to 1961, the share of export expansion as a source of growth was smaller for the labor-absorbing industries than for the other manufacturing industries. After 1961, however, the situation was reversed so that the labor-absorbing industries began to have more export expansion. The greatest effect of export expansion was observed in textiles and electrical machinery throughout the period 1961–76. We also note that the contribution of import substitution in the labor-absorbing category declined more rapidly and that changes in I-O coefficients of the two categories did not differ much.

Decomposition by Industry Group

The seven industry groups in Table 6.4 make up total manufacturing. Interesting results are observed as follows:

1. The greatest contribution of export expansion in the first period, 1956–61, was in food processing. However, it shifted to textiles after 1961, exceeding 100 percent from 1971 to 1976. Textiles still constitute the first-ranking exporting category.

Table 6.3   Sources of Manufacturing Output Growth
(by Degree of Labor Absorption)

(percent)

Period and Item	Domestic Demand Expansion	Export Ex-pansion	Import Substi-tution	Change in I-O Coefficients
1956-61				
Labor-absorbing				
manufacturing	52.0	27.9	14.3	5.8
Other manufacturing	39.2	41.8	12.6	6.4
Manufacturing total	44.3	36.3	13.2	6.2
1961-71				
Labor-absorbing				
manufacturing	32.8	58.4	5.1	3.7
Other manufacturing	42.4	42.3	10.8	4.5
Manufacturing total	36.9	51.5	7.6	4.0
1971-76				
Labor-absorbing				
manufacturing	16.5	82.7	0.8	—
Other manufacturing	26.6	76.1	− 2.7	—
Manufacturing total	19.8	80.6	− 0.4	—

Note:
  1. See Table 6.2, Note 1.
Sources: See Table 6.1.

Table 6.4   Sources of Manufacturing Output Growth
(by Industry Group)

(percent)

Period and Item	Domestic Demand Expansion	Export Ex- pansion	Import Substi- tution	Change in I-O Coefficients
1956-61				
Food processing	40.9	54.0	4.6	0.5
Textiles	56.0	37.4	0.6	6.0
Steel, iron, and its				
products	3.8	41.4	41.9	12.9
Electrical machinery	54.5	23.4	21.5	0.6
Machinery	67.3	17.6	13.0	2.1
Intermediate goods	34.7	28.4	27.9	9.0
Final goods	62.5	17.3	8.0	12.2
Manufacturing	44.3	36.3	13.2	6.2
1961-71				
Food processing	65.9	28.0	2.0	4.1
Textiles	24.4	64.7	8.0	2.9
Steel, iron, and its				
products	43.1	49.6	10.9	− 3.6
Electrical machinery	24.7	65.3	7.2	2.8
Machinery	54.7	30.8	9.0	5.5
Intermediate goods	43.1	42.1	8.1	6.7
Final goods	24.9	60.6	8.9	5.6
Manufacturing	36.9	51.5	7.6	4.0
1971-76				
Food processing	65.9	37.7	− 3.6	−
Textiles	− 12.2	103.8	8.4	−
Steel, iron, and its				
products	27.8	66.1	6.1	−
Electrical machinery	16.7	82.8	0.5	−
Machinery	52.0	58.5	− 10.5	−
Intermediate goods	57.0	57.2	− 14.2	−
Final goods	12.4	89.0	− 1.4	−
Manufacturing	19.8	80.6	− 0.4	−

Note:
1. See Table 6.2, Note 1.
Sources: See Table 6.1.

2. The increase in the export expansion contribution in electrical machinery was significant, as was that in final goods.
3. During the import substitution period of 1956–61, a high degree of import substitution was observed in steel, iron, and its products, intermediate goods, and electrical machinery.

Import Content in Domestic Demand and Exports

We know that final demand (domestic final demand plus exports) can be traced to two sources: domestic content and import content. The domestic content is the value added in the domestic economy, which constitutes the gross domestic product (GDP). The domestic content has three components: labor earnings, capital earnings, and indirect taxes. Import content refers to the amount or proportion of imported intermediate goods that are contained in final demand. The amount of import content is the amount of imported goods used to produce domestic final demand and exports. The portion of import content is the portion of imported intermediate goods used to produce each one dollar value of final demand. Thus, import content itself is not a component of GDP. However, it plays a great role in that the use of the imported materials and intermediate goods makes particular types of production possible. In this sense, appropriate imports are necessary for production and thus for the generation of domestic content and economic growth.

In this regard, we would like to study the status and change over time in import content in domestic final demand and exports and in import content as classified by industry.

Table 6.5 presents the distribution of imported intermediate goods used in production of domestic final demand and exports. In 1961, 77 percent of the imported intermediate goods were used in the production of domestic final demand and only 23 percent were used for exports.

However, in 1976, 63 percent of the imported intermediate goods were used in the production of exports, and exports of manufactures alone used 60 percent of the imported intermediates. Import content in exports to the United States grew most rapidly between 1961-76; 5 percent in 1961, it increased to 28 percent in 1976.

The share of import content in exports grew at a rapid rate because of a high rate of export expansion. At the same time, a rapid rate of export expansion was possible only because of a rapid increase in imports of intermediate goods. In previous sections, we have emphasized the importance of export opportunities for production—the importance on the market side. However, on the production side, the import of intermediates has been no less important. That is, had the imports not been available, the economy might not have grown as it did in the past. Thus, the opportunity to export was crucial in that exports broadened the market to provide more productive opportunities, at the same time making it possible to earn the foreign exchange necessary to import the materials and equipment needed for production.

Effects of Trade on Employment

One of the most important features of the economic development of the Republic of China was the achievement of full employment by 1971. In order to identify the contribution of exports to employment, sources of employment growth will be categorized as follows: domestic expansion, export expansion, import substitution, and technological change. Because the employment data in an input-output classification are available only after 1961 and because the rapid rise in the rate of labor absorption occurred after 1961, the decomposition of employment growth will be carried out only for 1961-76.

Creation of Job Opportunities

In the period 1961-76, employment in Taiwan increased

Table 6.5   Import Content in Domestic Final Demand
and Exports (as Percentage of Total Imports)

(percent)

Year and Industry	Import Content in Total Final Demand	Import Content in Domestic Final Demand	Import Content in Total Exports	Import Content in Exports to the U.S.
	TF	F^d	E	E_{us}
1961				
A-sector	6.4	5.6	0.8	0.1
M-sector	83.1	62.8	20.3	4.5
S-sector	6.8	5.2	1.6	0.4
Others	3.7	3.5	0.2	0.03
All sectors	100.0	77.1	22.9	5.0
1966				
A-sector	3.0	2.5	0.5	0.1
M-sector	81.4	48.8	32.6	7.0
S-sector	12.9	8.4	4.5	1.0
Others	2.7	2.4	0.3	0.1
All sectors	100.0	62.1	37.9	8.2
1971				
A-sector	3.3	2.5	0.8	0.1
M-sector	87.7	43.6	44.1	18.9
S-sector	6.5	4.3	2.2	0.9
Others	2.5	2.2	0.3	0.1
All sectors	100.0	52.6	47.4	20.0
1976				
A-sector	2.1	1.5	0.6	0.1
M-sector	90.8	30.6	60.2	27.4
S-sector	4.8	3.0	1.8	0.7
Others	2.3	1.9	0.4	0.1
All sectors	100.0	37.0	63.0	28.3

Note:
1. A, M, S stand for agricultural, manufacturing, and services sectors of industry.
Sources: Same as Table 6.1.

Import Content in Exports to Japan	Import Content in Exports to Asian Countries Other Than Japan	Import Content in Exports to Europe and Canada	Import Content in Exports to Other Places	Year and Industry
E_j	E_a	E_e	E_o	
				1961
0.3	0.2	0.1	0.1	A-sector
1.6	10.9	2.1	1.2	M-sector
0.4	0.6	0.1	0.1	S-sector
0.1	0.1	0.01	0.01	Others
2.4	11.8	2.3	1.4	All sectors
				1966
0.2	0.1	0.1	0.03	A-sector
2.0	17.1	3.0	3.5	M-sector
1.0	1.6	0.5	0.4	S-sector
0.1	0.1	0.04	0.03	Others
3.3	18.9	3.6	3.9	All sectors
				1971
0.4	0.1	0.1	0.1	A-sector
3.5	11.7	5.7	4.3	M-sector
0.3	0.5	0.3	0.2	S-sector
0.04	0.1	0.1	0.03	Others
4.2	12.4	6.2	4.6	All sectors
				1976
0.3	0.1	0.1	0.01	A-sector
5.8	9.2	10.1	7.7	M-sector
0.3	0.3	0.3	0.2	S-sector
0.04	0.1	0.1	0.1	Others
6.4	9.7	10.6	8.0	All sectors

by 2.3 million persons — 60 percent of the number employed in 1961. Such a sizable increase raises the questions of why and how those job opportunities were created.

The creation of job opportunities deals with two essential factors: labor productivity and output market. On the one hand, given a certain quantity of production, an advancement in labor productivity will reduce job opportunities. On the other hand, with labor productivity held constant, an expansion of output market will create job opportunities by increasing production opportunity. We also know that production opportunity is increased by expansion of domestic demand, expansion of exports, expansion due to import substitution, and technological change. Therefore, the number of job opportunities a society can really create is actually dependent on the algebraic sum of the above two elements, namely, the number reduced by the advancement of labor productivity and the number increased by the market expansion, as in the following equations:

$$L = \ell x$$

and

$$\Delta L = \ell \Delta X + X \Delta \ell$$

where
L = labor
X = output
$\ell = \dfrac{L}{X}$ = labor coefficient

Table 6.6 summarizes the results of the calculations that explain causes of employment expansion for the whole economy. From the second column in Table 6.6, we note that the continuous advancement in labor productivity over the fifteen-year period caused a continuous labor release. During 1961–66, the advancement in labor productivity caused labor demand to decrease by 1,824,000 persons, amounting to 49 percent of 1966 employment. The demand decrease in 1966–71 was 1,339,000, equivalent to 28 percent of 1971 employment; and that in 1971–76 was 1,681,000, equivalent to 30 percent of 1976 employment. It is obvious that if production opportunities had not expanded, the advancement of labor productivity would have created high unemployment. In other words, in the course of increasing productivity, market expansion for production expansion is a necessary condition for achieving and maintaining full employment.

The third column of Table 6.6 shows that the increase in labor demand due to market expansion was crucial for employment expansion over all three periods. During 1961–66, the market expansion (including domestic expansion, export expansion, import substitution, and change in input-output [I-O] coefficients] made labor demand increase by 2,201,000, amounting to 59 percent of 1966 employment. The increase in labor demand due to the market expansion was 2,354,000 in 1966–71, amounting to 49 percent of 1971 employment; and the increase in 1971–76 was 2,606,000, amounting to 46 percent of 1976 employment.

It is evident that the increase in job opportunities created by market expansion far exceeded the decrease in job opportunities caused by the advancement of productivity, so that net increases in employment of 377,000, 1,015,000, and 925,000, respectively, were generated for the three periods.

How was the market expanded? From Table 6.6 we know that in the first period, domestic expansion and export expansion accounted for 39 percent and 20 percent, respectively, of the 59 percent increase. The contribution to employment expansion from domestic expansion was about double that from export expansion in this early period. The contributions of import substitution and change in I-O coefficients were trivial. The importance of export expansion increased in the second period and continued to increase in the third period. The contribution to employment expansion from export expansion increased relatively in the second period. Thus, export expansion was the decisive factor that caused the economy to reach full employment in 1971. Furthermore, export expansion helped maintain this status after 1971. Employment expansion from export expansion

Table 6.6　Causes of Employment Expansion: An Aggregate
Observation, 1961- 1976

Period	Increment of Employment	Employment Release due to Advancement in Labor Productivity (A)	Employment Expansion due to Output Expansion (B)	Employment Expansion due to Domestic Expansion	Employment Expansion due to Exports Expansion
1961-66					
Increment in thousands	377	– 1,824	2,201	1,454	730
(Employment expansion in % of 1966 employment)	(10)	(– 49)	(59)	(39)	(20)
1966-71					
Increment in thousands	1,015	– 1,339	2,354	1,503	1,048
(Employment expansion in % of 1971 employment)	(21)	(– 28)	(49)	(32)	(22)
1971-76					
Increment in thousands	925	– 1,681	2,606	1,185	1,533
(Employment expansion in % of 1976 employment)	(16)	(– 30)	(46)	(21)	(27)

Note: A positive figure refers to an increase; a negative figure to a decrease.
Source: Based on calculation.

Employ- ment Expansion due to Exports to Developed Countries	Employ- ment Expansion due to Exports to Developing Countries	Change in Employ- ment due to Import Substitu- tion	Change in Employ- ment due to Change in I-O Coef- ficients	Period
				1961-66 Increment
402	328	− 10	27	in thousands
				(Employment expansion in % of 1966
(11)	(9)	(− 0.3)	(0.7)	employment)
				1966-71 Increment
786	262	− 21	− 176	in thousands
				(Employment expansion in % of 1971
(17)	(5)	(− 1)	(− 4)	employment)
				1971-76 Increment
1,172	361	− 112	−	in thousands
				(Employment expansion in % of 1976
(21)	(6)	(− 2)	−	employment)

in 1971–76 increased to account for 27 percent of 1976 employment, a very significant portion, of which 21 percent was generated by export expansion to the developed countries and the remaining 6 percent by export expansion to developing countries.

In Table 6.7, causes of employment expansion are listed by sectoral origin. We note that productivity in manufacturing advanced most rapidly, so the employment release due to the productivity advancement in manufacturing was the largest throughout the period 1961–76. But manufacturing also created the greatest number of job opportunities through export expansion. Particularly during the second and third periods, the employment increase due to export expansion in manufacturing was large enough to account for 60 percent of the total employment increase. That is, the employment opportunity created by export expansion was more than enough to compensate for the reduction made by the advancement in productivity so that total employment increased – absorbing not only the newcomers, but also those who were originally employed.

As for the agricultural sector in 1961–66, the increase in labor productivity reduced job opportunities by 44 percent, while domestic expansion and export expansion, respectively, contributed 32 percent and 14 percent. Therefore, employment increased slightly. The same tendency was observed for 1966–71. In the period 1971–76, although the speed of advancement in agricultural labor productivity slowed to reduce job opportunities by only 7 percent, the positive contributions of both domestic expansion and export expansion were not able to compensate for that decrease. As a result, agricultural employment decreased in absolute amount.

Because productivity in the agricultural sector is lower than that in the nonagricultural sector, the outmigration of the agricultural labor force to the nonagricultural sector tends to increase the average productivity of the whole economy on one hand, while raising the per household income of farmers on the other. Therefore, we consider the shift of the center of gravity from agriculture to nonagriculture a beneficial movement.

In short, the successful absorption of 2.3 million workers in the past fifteen years was attributable solely to market expansion. In the 1970s particularly, the contribution of export expansion far exceeded the contribution of domestic expansion.

Labor Utilization by Export Business

We have discussed how much export expansion contributed to increasing employment during a certain period of time. In this section we would like to examine how much labor is used for export business at a certain time. Therefore, instead of calculating the increase in employment, we shall examine the degree of labor utilization.

The allocation of labor utilization based on the input-output system is shown in Table 6.8. "Direct employment" refers to the direct utilization of labor, excluding the indirect effect. "Total employment" refers to the sum of direct and indirect employment, including the indirect effect. Accordingly, the ratio of total employment to direct employment measures the relative size of indirect employment induced by that particular sector.

Characteristics of the allocation of labor utilization are as follows:

1. A large portion of the labor force is used in the production of exports. The number of workers was 400,000 in 1961, comprising 11.9 percent of that year's employment; it increased to 1,924,000, comprising 34.0 percent, in 1976. In other words, in 1976 the export business provided 34 percent of employment opportunities.
2. The indirect effect of the production of export goods is greater than that of domestic goods. The production of exports to the developing countries in particular began to have a larger indirect effect after 1966.

Table 6.9 is a more detailed presentation of Table 6.8. Here labor utilization is allocated to the agriculture,

Table 6.7 Causes of Employment Expansion by
Industrial Origin, 1961—1976

Period and Industry	Incre- ment of Employ- ment	Employ- ment Release due to Advance- ment in Labor Produc- tivity	Employ- ment Expan- sion due to Output Expan- sion	Employ- ment Expan- sion due to Domestic Expan- sion	Employ- ment Expan- sion due to Exports Expan- sion
		(A)	(B)		
	(in thousands)	(%)	(%)	(%)	(%)
1961-66					
Agriculture	58	− 44	47	32	14
Manufacturing	139	− 93	117	51	50
Services	193	− 34	47	41	13
Whole economy	377	− 49	59	39	20
1966-71					
Agriculture	49	− 20	23	25	9
Manufacturing	493	− 53	99	29	59
Services	481	− 22	47	38	13
Whole economy	1,015	− 28	49	32	22
1971-76					
Agriculture	− 16	− 7	6	4	2
Manufacturing	516	− 42	74	15	60
Services	418	− 20	38	27	16
Whole economy	925	− 30	46	21	27

Notes:
1. 1961-66 increment of employment as % of 1966 employment;
2. 1966-71 increment of employment as % of 1971 employment;
3. 1971-76 increment of employment as % of 1976 employment.

Employment Expansion due to Exports to Developed Countries	Employment Expansion due to Exports to Developing Countries	Change in Employment due to Import Substitution	Change in Employment due to Change in I-O Coefficients	Period and Industry
(%)	(%)	(%)	(%)	
				1961-66
11	3	− 3	4	Agriculture
21	29	5	11	Manufacturing
7	6	0.3	− 7	Services
11	9	− 0.3	0.7	Whole economy
				1966-71
6	3	− 7	− 4	Agriculture
44	15	7	4	Manufacturing
10	3	0.2	− 4	Services
17	5	− 1	− 4	Whole economy
				1971-76
2	0	0.3	−	Agriculture
44	16	− 1	−	Manufacturing
12	4	− 5	−	Services
21	6	− 2	−	Whole economy

4. Services sector includes construction, electricity, gas, water and sanitary services.
Source: Based on calculation.

Table 6.8   Labor Utilization, Direct and Indirect, 1961—1976

(thousand)

Year	Labor Used by Total Final Demand	Labor Used by Domestic Final Demand	Labor Used by Total Exports	Labor Used by Exports to the Developed Countries	Labor Used by Exports to the Developing Countries
1961					
Total employment	3,353	2,953	400	238	162
Direct employment	1,920	1,739	181	105	76
Ratio of total employment to direct employment		1.70		2.27	2.13
1966					
Total employment	3,731	2,969	762	454	308
Direct employment	2,150	1,761	389	240	149
Ratio of total employment to direct employment		1.69		1.89	2.07
1971					
Total employment	4,746	3,523	1,223	836	387
Direct employment	2,923	2,241	682	489	193
Ratio of total employment to direct employment		1.57		1.71	2.01
1976					
Total employment	5,670	3,746	1,924	1,385	539
Direct employment	3,492	2,437	1,055	771	284
Ratio of total employment to direct employment		1.54		1.80	1.90

Source: Same as Table 6.7.

manufacturing, and services sectors. We note that in 1976 manufacturing exports utilized 18.2 percent of employment and that manufacturing exports to the developed countries alone provided 12.7 percent of employment. In economic theory, particularly in pure theory, services are often treated as "nontradables." In reality, services are also exported indirectly. For example, the employment opportunity provided by the exports of the services sector in 1976 reached as high as 10.5 percent of total employment, providing Taiwan's economy with 600,000 job opportunities.

The maintenance of full employment in the Republic of China currently depends greatly on the export business. Export business utilized 34 percent of total employment in 1976, with 5.3 percent in agricultural exports, 18.2 percent in manufacturing exports, and 10.5 percent in services.

The sources of value added and labor income are presented in Tables 6.10 and 6.11. As can be seen in the tables, the generation of value added and labor income is closely related to labor utilization. In 1961, value added induced by exports accounted for 12.2 percent of the total national income, and it increased to 34.8 percent in 1976. The same tendency is observed for labor earnings. Labor earnings from exports grew from 9.7 percent in 1961 to 36.1 percent in 1976. Here again we find the importance of exports in the course of economic growth in Taiwan.

Exports to the United States were the most important. In 1976, 12.3 percent of the national income was generated by exports to the United States, and 6.4 percent of the national income was generated by exports to Asian countries other than Japan. Exports to Europe and Canada contributed 6.0 percent to national income; exports to Japan contributed only 5.5 percent.

Exports were particularly important in manufacturing development, for in 1976 exports alone induced manufacturing industry to generate 20.2 percent of the national income, and exports accounted for 56 percent of total manufacturing income. The export of services contributed 10.3 percent to national income generation. The contribution of exports to the value added in the agricultural sector

Table 6.9   Allocation of Labor Utilization, 1961–1976

(percent)

Year and Industry	Labor Used by Total Final Demand	Labor Used by Domestic Final Demand	Labor Used by Total Exports
1961			
Agriculture	47.3	42.4	4.9
Manufacturing	13.3	9.7	3.6
Services	39.4	36.0	3.4
Whole economy	100.0	88.1	11.9
1966			
Agriculture	44.0	35.9	8.1
Manufacturing	15.7	9.3	6.4
Services	40.3	34.4	5.9
Whole economy	100.0	79.6	20.4
1971			
Agriculture	35.7	29.3	6.4
Manufacturing	22.7	10.7	12.0
Services	41.6	34.2	7.4
Whole economy	100.0	74.2	25.8
1976			
Agriculture	29.6	24.3	5.3
Manufacturing	28.1	9.9	18.2
Services	42.3	31.8	10.5
Whole economy	100.0	66.0	34.0

Source: Same as Table 6.7.

Labor Used by Exports to the Developed Countries	Labor Used by Exports to the U.S.	Labor Used by Exports to the Developing Countries	Year and Industry
			1961
3.4	1.0	1.5	Agriculture
1.8	0.9	1.8	Manufacturing
1.9	0.7	1.5	Services
7.1	2.6	4.8	Whole economy
			1966
6.1	1.4	2.0	Agriculture
2.9	1.5	3.5	Manufacturing
3.2	1.2	2.7	Services
12.2	4.1	8.2	Whole economy
			1971
4.7	1.1	1.7	Agriculture
8.0	5.1	4.0	Manufacturing
4.9	2.9	2.5	Services
17.6	9.1	8.2	Whole economy
			1976
4.3	1.0	1.0	Agriculture
12.7	7.0	5.5	Manufacturing
7.5	4.0	3.0	Services
24.5	12.0	9.5	Whole economy

Table 6.10   Structural Change in Value Added by Each Source
(Expressed as Percentage of Total Value Added)

Year and Industry	Value Added Induced by Total Final Demand	Value Added Induced by Domestic Final Demand	Value Added Induced by Total Exports	Value Added Induced by Exports to the U.S.
	TF	F^d	E	E_{us}
1961				
A-sector	28.5	25.2	3.3	0.6
M-sector	17.6	13.0	4.6	1.1
S-sector	46.1	42.5	3.6	0.8
Others	7.8	7.1	0.7	0.1
All sectors	100.0	87.8	12.2	2.6
1966				
A-sector	23.2	18.1	5.1	0.9
M-sector	22.6	15.2	7.4	1.4
S-sector	45.9	39.7	6.2	1.3
Others	8.3	6.8	1.5	0.3
All sectors	100.0	79.8	20.2	3.9
1971				
A-sector	15.0	11.6	3.4	0.7
M-sector	32.1	17.6	14.5	5.7
S-sector	45.3	37.3	8.0	3.2
Others	7.6	6.6	1.0	0.3
All sectors	100.0	73.1	26.9	9.9
1976				
A-sector	12.9	10.0	2.9	0.6
M-sector	36.2	16.0	20.2	7.2
S-sectors	42.3	32.0	10.3	4.0
Others	8.6	7.2	1.4	0.5
All sectors	100.0	65.2	34.8	12.3

Sources: Same as Table 6.1.

Value Added Induced by Exports to Japan	Value Added Induced by Exports to Asian Countries Other Than Japan	Value Added Induced by Exports to Europe and Canada	Value Added Induced by Exports to Other Places	Year and Industry
E_j	E_a	E_e	E_o	
				1961
1.4	0.8	0.2	0.3	A-sector
1.0	1.8	0.3	0.4	M-sector
1.0	1.2	0.3	0.3	S-sector
0.2	0.3	0.1	0.05	Others
3.6	4.1	0.9	1.0	All sectors
				1966
2.3	0.7	0.6	0.6	A-sector
0.7	3.7	0.8	0.8	M-sector
1.3	2.2	0.8	0.6	S-sector
0.3	0.7	0.1	0.1	Others
4.6	7.3	2.3	2.1	All sectors
				1971
1.4	0.6	0.6	0.1	A-sector
1.3	4.2	1.9	1.4	M-sector
0.9	1.9	1.3	0.7	S-sector
0.1	0.4	0.1	0.1	Others
3.7	7.1	3.9	2.3	All sectors
				1976
1.2	0.5	0.5	0.1	A-sector
2.6	4.0	3.4	3.0	M-sector
1.5	1.6	1.9	1.3	S-sector
0.2	0.3	0.2	0.2	Others
5.5	6.4	6.0	4.6	All sectors

Table 6.11   Structural Change in Labor Earnings by Each Source
(Expressed as Percentage of Total Labor Earnings)

Year and Industry	Labor Earnings Induced by Total Final Demand TF	Labor Earnings Induced by Domestic Final Demand F^d	Labor Earnings Induced by Total Exports E	Labor Earnings Induced by Exports to the U.S. E_{us}
1961				
A-sector	23.4	20.6	2.8	0.6
M-sector	9.2	6.8	2.4	0.5
S-sector	56.9	53.1	3.8	0.9
Others	10.5	9.8	0.7	0.1
All sectors	100.0	90.3	9.7	2.1
1966				
A-sector	18.9	14.9	4.0	0.7
M-sector	16.4	10.0	6.4	1.3
S-sector	53.2	46.2	7.0	1.5
Others	11.5	9.6	1.9	0.3
All sectors	100.0	80.7	19.3	3.8
1971				
A-sector	15.9	12.3	3.6	0.7
M-sector	23.4	11.7	11.7	4.9
S-sector	51.9	43.4	8.5	3.4
Others	8.8	8.0	0.8	0.2
All sectors	100.0	75.4	24.6	9.2
1976				
A-sector	5.1	3.6	1.5	0.3
M-sector	33.9	12.0	21.9	8.2
S-sector	49.9	38.4	11.5	4.5
Others	11.1	9.9	1.2	0.4
All sectors	100.0	63.9	36.1	13.4

Sources: Same as Table 6.1.

Labor Earnings Induced by Exports to Japan E_j	Labor Earnings Induced by Exports to Asian Countries Other Than Japan E_a	Labor Earnings Induced by Exports to Europe and Canada E_e	Labor Earnings Induced by Exports to Other Places E_o	Year and Industry
				1961
1.2	0.6	0.2	0.2	A-sector
0.4	1.0	0.2	0.3	M-sector
1.0	1.3	0.3	0.3	S-sector
0.2	0.3	0.1	0.04	Others
2.8	3.2	0.8	0.8	All sectors
				1966
1.9	0.5	0.5	0.4	A-sector
0.7	2.9	0.6	0.9	M-sector
1.5	2.4	0.9	0.7	S-sector
0.4	0.8	0.2	0.2	Others
4.5	6.6	2.2	2.2	All sectors
				1971
1.4	0.8	0.6	0.1	A-sector
1.0	3.0	1.7	1.1	M-sector
1.0	2.0	1.4	0.7	S-sector
0.1	0.3	0.1	0.1	Others
3.5	6.1	3.8	2.0	All sectors
				1976
0.8	0.1	0.2	0.1	A-sector
2.7	3.8	4.0	3.2	M-sector
1.7	1.8	2.1	1.4	S-sector
0.2	0.2	0.2	0.2	Others
5.4	5.9	6.5	4.9	All sectors

was relatively trivial, accounting for only 2.9 percent of the national income in 1976.

After the 1960s, export expansion was a decisive factor in rapid growth, and in the 1970s its importance outweighed even domestic expansion. In manufacturing, the contribution of export expansion in each trade pattern category has increased over time, particularly for the export competing industries, showing an increasing dependence on exports. After 1961, the labor-absorbing industries, particularly textiles and electrical machinery, showed the greatest export expansion, taking the place of food processing. Rapid export expansion was possible only because of an increase in imports of intermediate goods, and the share of import content in exports grew rapidly. Increased market opportunities abroad, particularly for labor-intensive products, created hundreds of thousands of jobs, despite advancements in labor productivity, enabling Taiwan to reach full employment.

7

The Impact of Taxation on Income Distribution

Today, it is generally understood that taxation should be used as a means to improve income distribution. Thus, all countries have adopted progressive income tax systems. However, not all taxes are progressive. Indirect taxes, such as commodity tax and customs duties, are mostly regressive. Therefore, we must examine carefully how a country's tax system affects its income distribution. If a country's indirect taxes are regressive, the favorable impact of direct taxes on income distribution may well be offset, at least in part, by the adverse impact of indirect taxes. Because of the difficulty in imputing the incidence of indirect taxes to each family, we will examine only the contribution of direct taxes to family income distribution in Taiwan. Naturally, if the contribution by direct taxes was very limited, then the addition of the adverse effect of indirect taxes would only worsen the situation.

Several comparisons will be made in order to address this problem. First, the ratio of income after income tax to income before income tax will be compared for various income groups. Second, effective rates of income tax for various income groups will be compared. Third, income inequality before direct tax and after direct tax will be compared.

Ratio of Incomes Before and After Income Tax

The ratio of incomes before and after income tax in each

137

income bracket can be used to measure the degree of tax progressiveness. The calculation is done separately for incomes in 1966 and 1972 in Table 7.1. We find that the degree of progressiveness in income taxes in Taiwan was significant. In 1966, for instance, for those families whose income was more than NT$1.5 million, income after taxes was reduced to 67.7 percent of the original, while those families whose incomes were less than NT$100,000 retained 98.2 percent of their original income. The same structure was observed for the year 1972, but the higher-income group paid an even higher percentage of income tax in 1972 than in 1966, while the lowest income group paid less.

Effective Rate of Tax

The effective rate of tax is one minus the percentage that appears in Table 7.1, indicating the rate of income tax that

Table 7.1   Ratio of Income After Income Tax to Income
Before Tax by Various Income Groups

(percent)

Income Group (thousands of NT dollars)	Total Individual Income 1966	Total Individual Income 1972
Under 100	98.2	98.8
100 – 300	95.5	93.1
300 – 500	90.3	87.8
500 – 800	85.0	82.0
800 – 1,500	78.3	74.9
Over 1,500	67.7	64.4
Average	70.5	66.4

Source: Ministry of Finance, file on income tax returns for 1972.

was actually applied to that particular income group. Comparing effective rates of income tax in 1972 with those in 1966 (see Table 7.2), we find that the structure of the effective rate changed in such a way that for the lowest income bracket the rates all decreased; for the higher income brackets the rates all increased. In this way, the changes can be said to be favorable to the improvement of income distribution.

Contribution of Direct Taxes to Income Distribution

From the above observations, we can see that the income tax system in Taiwan, the Republic of China, was progressive and had a favorable effect on income distribution. Here we would like to further examine how much levying direct taxes modified the inequality of income in the past. The question is whether the direct tax system in Taiwan

Table 7.2   Effective Rate of Income Tax by Income Groups

(percent)

Income Group (thousands of NT dollars)	Total Individual Income 1966	Total Individual Income 1972	Total Business Profit Income 1972	Total Salaries and Wages Income 1972	Total Other Incomes 1972
Under 100	1.8	1.2	1.2	1.3	0.9
100 – 300	4.5	6.9	6.8	6.6	6.9
300 – 500	9.7	12.2	12.7	11.7	12.4
500 – 800	15.0	18.0	18.5	17.6	17.5
800 – 1,500	21.7	25.1	25.4	24.5	24.8
Over 1,500	32.3	35.6	36.0	34.5	35.0
Average	29.5	33.6	34.6	29.3	31.1

Source: Same as Table 7.1.

contributed to the improvement of income distribution; and if so, by how much.

One convenient way to examine the impact of direct taxes on income distribution is to compare the Gini coefficients before taxes and after taxes. If the Gini coefficient is significantly lower after direct taxes are paid, we can say that taxation had a significant impact on the reduction of income inequality. Table 7.3 shows the Gini coefficients based on distribution before and after direct taxes. As can be seen in the table, the Gini coefficients after direct taxes are smaller than those before direct taxes for all years. This means that the direct taxes levied on families actually con-

Table 7.3   Gini Coefficients of Income Distribution
Before and After Direct Taxes, 1964–1978

Year	Gini Coefficient Before Direct Taxes (1)	Gini Coefficient After Direct Taxes (2)	Ratio of Gini Coefficient Before Tax to Gini Coefficient After Tax (1) / (2)
1964	0.3282	0.3275	1.002
1966	0.3301	0.3279	1.007
1968	0.3348	0.3309	1.012
1970	0.2991	0.2961	1.010
1972	0.2953	0.2912	1.014
1974	0.2996	0.2949	1.016
1976	0.2894	0.2845	1.017
1978	0.2888	0.2853	1.012

Sources: Department of Budget, Accounting and Statistics, Taiwan Provincial Government, *Report on the Survey of Family Income and Expenditure, Taiwan Province, Republic of China;* Bureau of Budget, Accounting and Statistics, Taipei City Government, *Report on the Survey of Family Income and Expenditure and Personal Income Distribution of Taipei City,* various years.

tributed to the reduction of income inequality in Taiwan. However, when we look at the relative magnitude of the two sets of coefficients, before taxes and after taxes, we find that the degree of reduction was so small that it ranged only from 0.002 percent to 0.017 percent. The reduction of the Gini coefficient in Taiwan during the period under observation (1964–78) was from 0.3282 to 0.2888, an annual decline of 0.9 percent on the average. Therefore, we may say that taxation was not a major cause of reduction in income inequality during this period and that other factors, which have been analyzed in the previous chapters, must have contributed more to the improvement of income distribution.

8
Conclusions

The ultimate purpose of an examination of the Republic of China's development experience should be more than simply an attempt to understand what happened during a specified period. It should be to distill conclusions that may be relevant to other developing societies and to determine special features that are likely to be irrelevant elsewhere.

At the aggregate level, the most important, if general, policy conclusion that may be derived from our work is this:

It is possible for economic growth to be compatible with an improved distribution of income during every phase of the transition from colonialism to a modern developed economy.

Taiwan's experience demonstrates that if assets are not distributed too unequally, this result can be achieved by following a growth path that consists initially of a flexible version of primary import substitution and later allows relative factor and commodity prices to better reflect changes over time in the availability of resources and production factors. True, few other developing countries have the same combination of a relatively favorable initial distribution of assets and a willingness to deploy the market mechanism effectively over time. But the experience in Taiwan does not support those who argue that because tinkering with relative prices did not work in the 1950s and 1960s, we must now adopt radical measures. Nor does it support the argument that the market solution at every step of the way, in the presence of powerful landed or industrial interests, will yield the desired complementarity between the objectives of growth and equity. What it does support is the conclusion that, given initial conditions that are not too unfavorable, such complementarity can be achieved by shaping the basic growth path, not by following what may be called a secondary or mop-up strategy through direct interventions by government. That is, such complementarity can be achieved by following a different primary strategy of transition growth. The basic thesis of this volume, then, is that an equitable level of income distribution can come about mainly through the *kind* of economic growth that is generated and, hence, that income distribution policy should center on growth-related policies.

Economic development in Taiwan has been characterized by *industrialization* and *labor intensiveness.* That is, successful labor absorption and growth have been possible, first, because of rapid industrialization and, second, because of Taiwan's relatively labor-intensive strategy.

Industrialization shifted the economy from agriculturally oriented production, which is by nature less productive than manufacturing and is incapable of absorbing more labor, and raised the economy to an "improved" status: The average productivity and labor-absorbing capacity of the entire economy became much higher than previously. Thus, the larger role of the nonagricultural sector can be considered one of the most essential factors in labor absorption and economic growth.

A labor-intensive strategy was important in that it played the following three roles during the course of development:

1. It made it possible to absorb more labor.
2. Light industries made the production of manufactured goods possible due to their simple technologies and limited use of capital.
3. On the demand side, labor-intensive outputs made it possible for Taiwan to compete in the world market

because its exports had a higher labor content at a lower labor cost than those of its competitors. The role played by exports in Taiwan's economic development can be understood in this context.

Our study found that exports were an important factor in the success of labor-intensive industrialization. Export opportunities were crucial: They broadened the market, thereby providing more production opportunities, and they simultaneously earned the foreign exchange necessary for importing the materials and equipment needed for further production.

After 1961, export expansion increased rapidly and made an increasingly large contribution to the economy in general and the manufacturing sector in particular. Exports were the primary source of manufacturing growth after the 1960s. For the economy as a whole, they were the essential factor in its rapid growth, successful absorption of labor, and improved income distribution over the past ten years or so.

The growth of Taiwan's exports to developed countries was much faster than that to developing countries. Because production for export to developed countries employed relatively labor-intensive technology, an abundant labor force was utilized efficiently and the economy reached a full-employment status by 1971. This in turn contributed to a more equitable income distribution by raising the incomes of lower-income groups and by providing farmers an opportunity to earn nonagricultural income.

Government policies are considered to have been essential in Taiwan's successful development. The government's stabilization policies, based on monetary reform, high interest rates, and so on, proved decisive. In the early 1950s, government policies stimulated import substitution. Land reform and rice-pricing policies contributed to limiting the production and export of rice and stimulated agricultural diversification. A multiple foreign exchange rate system was carefully and successfully transformed into a unitary exchange system in 1961, and U.S. aid was efficiently utilized.

From the 1950s on, export promotion was emphasized. Various export promotion schemes were implemented, including the main ones discussed in this study: trade policy (including the exchange rate and the nominal rate of protection), investment policy, tax refunds, loan policy, and government expenditures on education.

Despite all this, Taiwan's future development and labor-absorption capacity is a major concern because the country's economy is at a turning point. On the one hand, unskilled labor has now been virtually fully utilized and wage rates have been going up. On the other hand, there is an abundance of college and high school graduates. Furthermore, many newcomers in the world market are producing at lower wage rates than Taiwan, protectionism is growing all over the world, and the price of oil will continue to be high.

Given this new set of circumstances, the strategy for future development should be carefully planned. The following points must be taken into consideration:

- Low energy intensiveness
- High technology intensiveness
- High value added
- High skilled-labor intensiveness
- High marketability
- Strong defense foundation
- High domestic linkage

Among the manufacturing industries, machinery and electronics best meet all these conditions. Upgraded textiles are also an important industry for the future. In the service sector, banking and finance have been of increasing importance in recent years and will continue to be so. The computer industry is developing fast. All of these are strategic industries for future development. A number of related laws, regulations, and tariffs should be revised, and other measures should be taken to promote these strategic industries. These are the prerequisites to continued economic expansion and development. The necessary adjustments in industrial production and government policy must be made quickly if Taiwan is to continue to carry out successful development plans that will produce both rapid growth and improved distribution.

Notes

Chapter 1

1. Simon Kuznets, "Economic Growth and Income Inequality," *American Economic Review*, Vol. 45 (March 1955), pp. 1–28; idem, "Quantitative Aspects of the Economic Growth of Nations: VIII, Distribution of Income by Size," *Economic Development and Cultural Change*, Vol. 11 (1963), pp. 1–80; Felix Paukert, "Income Distribution at Different Levels of Development: A Survey of Evidence," *International Labour Review*, Vol. 108 (August and September 1973), pp. 97–124; Irma Adelman and Cynthia Taft Morris, *Economic Growth and Social Equity in Developing Countries* (Stanford, Calif.: Stanford University Press, 1973).

Chapter 2

1. The speed of industrialization is compared with the corresponding period of 1952–69 for Taiwan's economy and 1860–1913 for other economies.

2. G. Ranis and J.C.H. Fei, "Innovation, Capital Accumulation, and Economic Development," *American Economic Review*, Vol. 53 (June 1963), p. 283; see also idem, *Development of the Labor Surplus Economy: Theory and Policy* (Homewood, Ill.: Richard D. Irwin, 1964).

3. Shirley W. Y. Kuo, "Economic Growth and Structural Change in the Republic of China" (World Bank, 1979; mimeo); idem, "Technical Change, Foreign Investment, and Growth in Taiwan's Manufacturing Industries, 1952–1970," in Shinichi Ichimura, ed., *The Economic Development of East and Southeast Asia* (Honolulu: University Press of Hawaii, 1975).

4. You-tsao Wang and Yueh-eh Chen, "Secular Trends of Out-

put, Inputs and Productivity: A Quantitative Analysis of Agricultural Development in Taiwan," *Conference on Agricultural Development in China, Japan and Korea* (Taipei: Academia Sinica, Graduate Institute of Economics, December 1980).

5. Shirley W. Y. Kuo, "Labor Absorption in Taiwan, 1954–1971," *Economic Essays*, Vol. 7 (Taipei: National Taiwan University, Graduate Institute of Economics, 1977).

6. Kuo, "Technical Change."

7. S. Kuznets, "Economic Growth and Income Inequality," *American Economic Review*, Vol. 45 (March 1955), pp. 1–28; idem, "Quantitative Aspects of the Economic Growth of Nations."

8. H. Chenery, M. S. Ahluwalia, C.L.G. Bell, J. H. Duloy, and R. Jolly, *Redistribution with Growth* (London: Oxford University Press, 1974).

9. William Nordhaus and James Tobin, *Is Growth Obsolete?* Economic Growth 50th Anniversary Colloquium, National Bureau of Economic Research (New York: Columbia University Press, 1972); Paul A. Samuelson, *Economics*, 9th ed. (New York: McGraw-Hill, 1973), pp. 195–197; report (in Japanese) by the Net National Welfare Committee of the Economic Council of Japan (Tokyo, 1973).

Chapter 3

1. Kowie Chang, "An Estimate of Taiwan Personal Income Distribution in 1953: Pareto's Formula Discussed and Applied," *Journal of Social Science*, Vol. 7 (August 1956); National Taiwan University, College of Law, "Report on Pilot Study of Personal Income and Consumption in Taiwan" (prepared under the sponsorship of a working group of National Income Statistics, Directorate-General of Budget, Accounting and Statistics [DGBAS]; processed in Chinese).

2. Chang, "Estimate of Taiwan Personal Income Distribution in 1953"; National Taiwan University, "Report on Pilot Study."

3. Joint Commission on Rural Reconstruction, "Taiwan Farm Income Survey of 1967: With a Brief Comparison with 1952, 1957, and 1962," *Economic Digest Series*, no. 20 (Taipei: Joint Commission on Rural Reconstruction, 1970).

4. The quality of the data, particularly for the 1950s, is suspect. Calculation of total personal income in 1953 by ag-

gregating the product of average family income and the number of households in each income group gives a figure 20 percent lower than that of the national accounts data. A similar calculation found that the 1953 data underestimated the total family income given in the national accounts data by 16.7 percent, but that the 1959 data overestimated total family income by 15.3 percent. The 1964 DGBAS data were found to underestimate total family income by only about 5 percent.

Although more than half of Taiwan's population in 1953 was in agriculture, 84 percent of the 1953 sample group came from the more urbanized and industrialized areas; 58 percent of that group lived in Taiwan's four largest cities. If rural income was better distributed than urban income, as was seen earlier, any overweighting of urban income may have resulted in a low estimate of total personal income and a high estimate of the Gini coefficient. In turn, although DGBAS data for 1964 did not include an appropriate number of families with income exceeding NT$200,000, the downward bias in the Gini is probably too small to be of much importance. Nevertheless, the survey results for the 1950s must be accepted with caution.

With respect to the underestimation of income distribution inequality—the 1964 Gini coefficient based on decile groups is 0.328—households with income exceeding NT$200,000 accounted for only 0.1 percent of the population and 1.15 percent of total income. Even if the income share of these households is increased by 1 percentage point, which would almost double their income share, and if the 1 percent loss is equally assigned to the first nine decile groups, the Gini coefficient would increase by only 3.1 percent to 0.3307. The increase really is not that large. To give an idea of the effect of the underestimation of the Gini coefficient, again for the 1964 data, suppose the income share of the top decile group to be increased by 2, 3, and 4 percentage points. Then the Gini coefficients would rise by 6.2 percent, 9.3 percent, and 12.4 percent to 0.3406, 0.3505, and 0.3604, respectively. Thus, the smaller the population, income share, underestimation of the wealthiest households, or any combination of these elements, the smaller the downward bias of the Gini coefficient.

5. Economic Planning Council, *Taiwan Statistical Data Book, 1975* (Taipei: Economic Planning Council, 1975), pp. 48, 53–55.

6. Ibid., p. 58.

7. The discussion of land reform draws heavily on Samuel P. S. Ho, *Economic Development in Taiwan: 1860–1970* (New Haven: Yale University Press, 1978), and Chao-Chen Cheng, "Land Reform and Agricultural Development in Taiwan" (paper read at Conference on Economic Development of Taiwan, June 19–28, 1967, Taipei; processed).

8. In 1945 and 1946, 640,000 mainlanders moved to Taiwan. Kuang Lu, "Population and Employment," in *Economic Development of Taiwan*, ed. Kowie Chang (Taipei: Cheng Chung Books, 1968), p. 532.

9. Chao-Chen Cheng, *Land Reform in Taiwan* (Taipei: China Publishing, 1961), p. 310.

10. Ibid., p. 309.

11. Individual landowners were allowed to retain three chia of medium-grade land. Anthony Y. C. Koo, *The Role of Land Reform in Economic Development: A Case Study of Taiwan* (New York: Frederick A. Praeger, 1968), p. 38.

12. Ho, *Economic Development in Taiwan*, p. 166.

13. T. Martin Yang, *Socio-Economic Results of Land Reform in Taiwan* (Honolulu: East-West Center, 1970).

14. T. H. Lee and T. H. Shen, "Agriculture as a Base for Socio-Economic Development," in *Agriculture's Place in the Strategy of Development*, ed. T. H. Shen (Taipei: Joint Commission on Rural Reconstruction, 1974), p. 300.

15. Deposits of the credit divisions of farmers' associations increased from about NT$100 million to NT$2,700 million by the end of 1965. Loans increased commensurately. Wen-Fu Hsu, "The Role of Agricultural Organizations in Agricultural Development" (paper read at Conference on Economic Development of Taiwan, June 19–28, 1967, Taipei; processed). Also during this period, credit became available to farmers from the JCRR, government-owned banks, and government agencies and monopolies. Between 1949 and 1960 the proportion of farm loans provided through the organized money market rose from 17 percent to 57 percent. Ho, *Economic Development in Taiwan*, pp. 179–80.

16. Ho estimated that 44.9 percent of the growth of agricultural output during 1951–60 can be attributed to changes in total factor productivity: 10.3 percent to increases in crop area and 34.7 percent to increases in working capital. Ho, *Economic Development in Taiwan*, pp. 147–85.

17. Ibid., p. 178.

18. Yujiro Hayami and Vernon W. Ruttan, *Agricultural Development in International Perspective* (Baltimore: Johns Hopkins University Press, 1971), passim.

19. You-tsao Wang, "Agricultural Development," in Chang, *Economic Development of Taiwan*, p. 176.

20. W. H. Lai, "Trend of Agricultural Employment in Post-War Taiwan" (paper read at Conference on Manpower in Taiwan, 1972, Taipei; processed).

21. The estimation difficulties here are well known, and we do not place much confidence in these numbers.

22. Ho, *Economic Development in Taiwan*, p. 158. Ho derived his figures from S. F. Liu, "Disguised Unemployment in Taiwan Agriculture" (Ph.D. dissertation, University of Illinois, 1966), and Paul K. C. Liu, "Economic Development and Population in Taiwan since 1895: An Overview," in *Essays on the Population of Taiwan* (Taipei: Academia Sinica, Graduate Institute of Economics, 1973).

23. Ho, *Economic Development in Taiwan*, p. 597.

24. Council on U.S. Aid, *Industry of Free China*, Vol. 1, no. 4 (1954).

25. Economic Planning Council, *Taiwan Statistical Data Book, 1975* (Taipei: Economic Planning Council, 1975), p. 28.

26. See Carlos F. Diaz-Alejandro, "On the Import Intensity of Import Substitution," *Kyklos*, Vol. 18 (1965).

27. Chang, *Economic Development in Taiwan*.

28. T. H. Lee, *Intersectoral Capital Flows in the Economic Development of Taiwan, 1895–1960* (Ithaca, N.Y.: Cornell University Press, 1971).

29. C. Y. Lin, *Industrialization in Taiwan, 1946–1972* (New York: Praeger Publishers, 1973).

Chapter 4

1. See Shirley W. Y. Kuo, "Economic Growth and Structural Change in the Republic of China" (World Bank, 1979; mimeo.).

Chapter 5

1. John C. H. Fei, Gustav Ranis, and Shirley W. Y. Kuo, *Growth with Equity: The Taiwan Case* (London: Oxford University Press, 1979).

2. Mathematically, the functional distribution effect and fac-

tor Gini effect can be explained as follows. Differentiating equation 5.1 with respect to time t gives:

$$\frac{dG_y}{dt} = (G_w - G_\pi)d\phi_w + \phi_\pi dG_\pi + \phi_w dG_w$$

$(G_w - G_\pi)d\phi_w$ is the functional distribution effect, and $\phi_\pi dG_\pi$ + $\phi_w dG_w$ is the factor Gini effect.

3. Directorate-General of Budget, Accounting and Statistics, "Report on the Survey of Family Income and Expenditure," 1964, 1966, 1970, 1972, 1974, 1976 and 1978.

4. Fei et al., Growth with Equity.

5. S. Kuznets, "Demographic Components in Size Distribution of Income," in Income Distribution, Employment and Economic Development in Southeast and East Asia, Vol. 2 (Tokyo: Japan Economic Research Center, 1975), pp. 389–472.

6. In the DGBAS family survey, a farm family refers to a family the head of which is registered as a farmer; accordingly, the farm-family income includes all incomes received by the farm family, from both agricultural and nonagricultural activities.

7. Yen Hwa, "The Female Labor Force of Taiwan: Tapping a New Resource," Conference on Population and Economic Development in Taiwan (Taipei: Academia Sinica, Graduate Institute of Economic Research, December 29, 1975–January 2, 1976).

Index

Adelman, Irma, 1
Agriculture, 2, 3, 12
  associations, 55–56
  capital in, 47–48
  credit, 55
  development of, 46–60
  diversification in, 58,
    59(chart), 145
  employment in, 12, 15(table),
    47(table), 58, 60, 104, 124,
    130–131(table)
  exports, 23, 56, 129, 136.
    See also Food processing
    industry, exports
  extension programs, 55
  and fertilizer use, 48
  and flood control, 48
  and government policies, 56,
    58
  and gross domestic product
    (GDP), 9–10
  imports, 27(chart)
  income, 54–55. *See also*
    Wage income, rural
  institutional infrastructure,
    55–56
  and irrigation, 43, 48
  and labor-intensive crops, 58
  and pesticide use, 48, 56
  population in, 46
  pricing policies, 56, 58, 60
  productivity in, 16, 17–19,
    46–47, 50, 57(table), 124

  technology in, 48, 53, 56
  wages in, 21(chart). *See also*
    Wage income, rural
  working days in, 58
    See also Food processing
    industry; Livestock
    production; Taiwan, land
    reform
Asparagus, 11, 56, 58

Bank of Taiwan, 66, 67

Canada, 8, 9(chart). *See also*
  Taiwan, and Canada
Capital
  accumulation, 16
  goods imports, 27(chart), 63
  private ownership of, 62
Chemical industry, 30
Chenery, H., 31
Chia, 50
China, Republic of. *See* Taiwan
Commodity tax, 77, 137
Consumer goods imports,
  27(chart)
Cotton, 47, 68
Critical minimum effort, 16
Customs duties, 77, 137

Demand, 109–110, 116,
  132–133(table)

155